THE
IRRATIONAL
IN
POLITICS

THE
IRRATIONAL
IN
POLITICS

by Maurice Brinton

BLACK ROSE BOOKS ——— Montréal

Copyright 1974 ©

Maurice Brinton

Published in mimeograph form by SOLIDARITY,
123 Lathon Road, E. 6, ENGLAND.

BLACK ROSE BOOKS No. D 16

First Edition 1974

Hardcover ...... ISBN : 0-919618-75-8

Paperback ...... ISBN : 0-919618-24-3

Canadian Shared Cataloguing in Publication Data

Brinton, Maurice.
 The irrational in politics / by Maurice
Brinton. — Montreal : Black Rose Boocks, c1974.
                    (Black rose books ; no. D16)

1. Political psychology. 2. Political participation.
I. Title.

JA74.5B73   301.5'92
ISBN 0-919618-75-8
ISBN 0-919618-24-3 (pbk.)

BLACK ROSE BOOKS LTD.

3934 St. Urbain

Montréal 131, Québec

Printed and bound in Québec, Canada

CONTENTS

Introduction 9

Examples of the Irrational 12

Some Inadequate Explanations 15

The Ignored Area and the Traditional Left 18

The Process of Conditioning 22

The Function of the Family 26

The Historical Roots 32

Wilhelm Reich and the Sexual Revolution 39

Limits and Perspectives 45

The Russian Experience 49

Appendix 1 : Women, Marriage and Sex from
              « Reminiscences of Lenin » by
              Clara Zetkin 64

Appendix 2 : Excerpt from
              « Memoirs of a Revolutionary
              1901-1941 » by Victor Serge 71

Introduction

"Propagnada and policemen, prisons and schools, traditional values and traditional morality all serve to reinforce the power of the few and to convince or coerce the many into acceptance of a brutal, degrading and irrational system."

from AS WE SEE IT [1]

This book is an attempt to analyse the various mechanisms whereby modern society manipulates its slaves into accepting their slavery and — at least in the short term — seems, to succeed. It does not deal with 'police' and 'jail' as ordinarily conceived but with those internalised patterns of repression and coercion, and with those intellectual prisons in which the 'mass individual' is today entrapped.

9

The book starts by giving a few examples of irrational behaviour — at the level of politics — of classes, groups and individuals. It proceeds to reject certain facile 'interpretations' put forward to explain these phenomena. It probes the various ways in which the soil (the individual psyche of modern man) has been rendered fertile (receptive) for an authoritarian, hierarchical and class-dominated culture. It looks at the family as the locus of reproduction of the dominant ideology, and at sexual repression as an important determinant of social conditioning, resulting in the mass production of individuals perpetually craving authority and leadership and forever afraid of walking on their own or of thinking for themselves. Some of the problems of the developing sexual revolution are then discussed. The book concludes by exploring a new dimension in the failure of the Russian Revolution. Throughout, the aim is to help people acquire additional insight into their own psychic structure. The fundamental desires and aspirations of the ordinary individual, so long distorted and repressed, are in deep harmony with an objective such as the libertarian reconstruction of society. The revolutionary 'ideal must therefore be made less remote and abstract. It must be shown to be the fulfilment — starting here and now — of people's own independent lives.

The book consists of two essays : *'The Irrational in Politics'* and *'The Russian Experience'*. These can be read independently. The subject matter does not overlap although the main arguments interlock at several levels. The essays are followed by 2 appendices. The first is an excerpt from Clara Zetkin's *'Reminiscences of Lenin'*. It illustrates an aspect of Lenin's thinking little known — or deliberately 'forgotten' — by all those Leninists now jumping onto the band-wagon of women's liberation. The second, an excerpt from Victor Serge's *'Memoirs of a Revolutionary'*, describes the Chubarov Alley Affair, a grim episode of the Russia of 1926.

Frequent references will be found in this book to the works of Wilhelm Reich. This should not be taken to imply that I subscribe to all that Reich wrote — a point spelled out in fuller and more specific detail on page 39. In the area that concerns us Reich's most relevant works were written in the early 1930s. At that time, although critical of developments in Russia (and more critical still of the policy of the German Communist Party) Reich still subscribed to many of their common fundamental

---

(1.) AS WE SEE IT is basic statement of principles of the revolutionary group, SOLIDARITY.
(2.) See *'The Sexual Revolution'*, (The Noonday Press, New York 1962), p. 204.

assumptions. Even later he still spoke of the 'basic socialism of the Soviet Union' [2] and muted his criticisms of the Bolshevik leaders to an extent that is no longer possible for us, writing four decades later. Moreover such is the influence of authoritarian conditioning that even those who have achieved the deepest insight into its mechanisms cannot fully escape its effects. There is an undoubted authoritarian strand in Reich. [3]

A final point concerns the section on the historical roots of sexual repression. The author (who is neither a historian nor an anthropologist) found this difficult to write. There seems little doubt, on the evidence available, that sexual repression arose at a specific point in time and fulfilled a specific social function — although experts differ as to many of the details. The difficulty here has been to steer a middle course between the great system-builders of the 19th century — who tended to 'tidy up reality' in order to make it conform with their grandiose generalisations — and the theoretical nihilism of many contemporary social scientists who refuse to see the wood for the trees. For instance the reluctance of Establishment anthropologists to envisage their subject from an historical viewpoint often stems, one suspects, from fear of the revolutionary implications of such an approach and of its implicit threat to contemporary institutions. We share none of these fears and can therefore look into this area without it generating either anxiety or hostile reactions.

(3.) See for instance the recent biography by his third wife, Ilse Ollendorf, referred to on page 39.

Examples of the Irrational

For anyone interested in politics the "irrational" behaviour of individuals, groups or large sections of the population looms as an unpleasant, frightening, but incontrovertible fact. Here are a few examples.

Between 1914 and 1918 millions of working people slaughtered one another in the 'war to end wars'. They died for ends that were not theirs, defending the interests of their respective rulers. Those who had nothing rallied to their respective flags and butchered one another in the name of 'Kaiser' or 'King and Country'. Twenty years later the process was repeated, on an even vaster scale.

In the early 1930s the economic crisis hit Germany. Hundreds of thousands were out of work and many were hungry. Bourgeois society revealed its utter incapacity even to provide the elementary material needs of men. The time was ripe for radical change. Yet at this crucial juncture millions of men and women (including very substantial sections of the German working class) preferred to follow the crudely nationalistic, self-contradictory (anti-capitalist and anti-communist) exhortations of a reactionary demagogue, preaching a mixture of racial hatred, puritanism and ethnological nonsense, rather than embark on the unknown road of social revolution. [1]

In New Delhi in 1966 hundreds of thousands of half-starving Indian peasants and urban poor actively participated in the biggest and most militant demonstration the town had ever known. Whole sections of the city were occupied, policemen attacked, cars and buses burnt. The object of this massive action was not, however, to protest against the social system which maintained the vast mass of the people in a state of permanent poverty and made a mockery of their lives. It was to denounce some contemplated legislation permitting cow slaughter under specific circumstances. Indian 'revolutionaries' meanwhile were in no position to make meaningful comment. Did they not still allow their parents to fix their marriages for them and considerations of caste repeatedly to colour their politics ?

In Britian several million working people, disappointed with the record of the Labour Government, with its wage freeze and attempted assault on the unions, voted Conservative. As they did in 1930. And in 1950-51. Or, to the unheard tune of encouragement from self-styled revolutionaries, they will vote Labour, expecting (or not) that things will be 'different next time'.

At a more mundane level the behaviour of consumers today is no more 'rational' than that of voters or of the oppressed classes in history. Those who understand the roots of popular

---

(1.) The popular vote for Nazi candidates in the last stages of the Weimar Republic increased from 800,000 in May 1928 to 6½ million in September 1930. (See A. Rosenberg 'A History of the German Republic' (Methuen, 1936) pp. 275, 304.)

preference know how easily demand can be manipulated. Advertising experts are fully aware that rational choice has little to do with consumer preferences. When a housewife is asked why she prefers one product to another the reasons she gives are seldom the real ones (even if she is answering in total good faith).

Largely unconscious motives even influence the ideas of revolutionaries and the type of organisation in which they choose to be active. At first sight it might appear paradoxical that those aspiring to a non-alienated and creative society based on equality and freedom should 'break' with bourgeois conceptions ... only to espouse the hierarchical, dogmatic, manipulatory and puritanical ideas of Leninism. It might appear odd that their 'rejection' of the irrational and arbitrarily imposed behaviour patterns of bourgeois society, with its demands for uncritical obedience and acceptance of authority, should take the form of that epitome of alienated activity : following the tortuous 'line' of a vanguard Party. It might seem strange that those who urge people to think for themselves and to resist the brainwashing of the mass media should be filled with anxiety whenever new ideas raise their troublesome heads within their own ranks. [2] Or that revolutionaries today should still seek to settle personal scores through resort to the methods prevailing in the bourgeois jungle outside. But, as we shall show, there is an internal coherence in all this apparent irrationality.

---

[2] We have recently heard it quite seriously proposed in an allegedly libertarian organisation — our own — that no one should speak on behalf of the organisation before submitting the substance of his proposed comments to a 'meetings committee', lest anything new be suddenly sprung on the unsuspecting and presumably defenceless ranks of the ideologically emancipated.

Some inadequate explanations

Confronted with disturbing facts like mass popular support for imperialist wars or the rise of fascism, a certain type of traditional revolutionary can be guaranteed to provide a stereotyped answer. He will automatically stress the 'betrayal' or 'inadequacy' of the Second or Third Internationals, or of the German Communist Party . . . or of this or that leadership which, for some reason or other, failed to rise to the historical occasion. (People who argue in this way don't even seem to appreciate that the repeated *tolerance* by the masses of such 'betrayals' or 'inadequacies' itself warrants a serious explain-ation.)

More sophisticated revolutionaries will lay the blame else-where. The means of moulding public opinion (press, radio, TV, churches, schools and universities) are in the hands of the ruling class. These media consequently disseminate ruling class ideas, values and priorities — day in, day out. What is dissemi-nated affects all layers of the population, contaminating everyone. Is it surprising, these revolutionaries will ask with a withering smile, that under such circumstances the mass of the people still retain reactionary ideas ? [1]

This explanation, although partially correct, is insufficient. In the long run it will not explain the continued acceptance by the working class of bourgeois rule — or that such rule has only been overthrown to be replaced by institutions of state capitalist type, embodying fundamentally similar hierarchical re-lationships (cult of the leader, total delegation of authority to an 'elite' Party, worship of revealed truth to be found in sacred texts or in the edicts of the Central Committee). If — both East and West — millions of people cannot face up to the implications of their exploitation, if they cannot perceive their enforced intellectual and personal under-development, if they cannot bear to look at the emptiness of their lives, if they are unaware of the intrinsically repressive character of so much that they consider 'rational', 'common sense', 'obvious', or 'natural' (hierarchy, inequality and the puritan ethos, for instance), if they are afraid of initiative and of self-activity, afraid of thinking new thoughts and of treading new paths, and if they are ever ready to follow this leader or that (promising them the moon), or this Party or that (undertaking to change the world 'on their behalf') , it is because there are powerful factors conditioning their behaviour from a *very early age* and inhibiting their accession to a different kind of consciousness.

Let us consider for a moment — and not through rose-tinted spectacles — the average British middle-aged working class voter today (it matters little in this respect whether he votes 'Conservative' or 'Labour'. He is probably hierarchy- cons-cious, xenophobic, racially-prejudiced, pro-monarchy, pro-capital punishment, pro-law and order, anti-demonstrator, anti-long haired student and anti-drop out. He is almost certainly sexually repres-sed (and hence an avid, if vicarious, consumer of the distorted

---

(1.) To accept this as an 'explanation' would be to vest in ideas a power they cannot have, namely the power totally to dominate material conditions, neutralising the influence of the economic facts of life. It is surprising that this should never have occurred to our 'marxists'.

sexuality endlessly depicted in the pages of the *News of the World).* No 'practical' Party (aiming at power through the ballot-box) would ever dream of appealing to him through the advocacy of wage equality, workers' management of production, racial integration, penal reform, abolition of the monarchy, dissolution of the police, sexual freedom for adolescents or the legalisation of pot. Anyone proclaiming this kind of 'transitional programme' would not only fail to get support but would probably be considered some kind of a nut.

But there is an even more important fact. Anyone trying to discuss matters of this kind will almost certainly meet not only disbelief but also that positive hostility that often denotes latent anxiety. [2] One doesn't meet this kind of response if one argues various meaningless or downright ludicrous propositions. Certain subjects are clearly emotionally loaded. Discussing them generates peculiar resistances that are hardly amenable to rational argument.

It is the purpose of this book to explore the nature and cause of these resistances and to point out that they are not innate but socially determined. (If they were innate, there would be no rational or socialist perspective whatsoever.) We will be led to conclude that these resistances are the result of a long-standing conditioning, going back to earliest childhood, and that this conditioning is mediated through the already conditioned parents and through the whole institution of the patriarchal family. The net result is a powerful reinforcement and perpetuation of the dominant ideology and the mass production of individuals with slavery built into them, individuals ready at a later stage to accept the authority of school teacher, priest, employer and politician (and to endorse the prevailing pattern of 'rationality'). Understanding this collective character structure gives one new insight into the frequently 'irrational' behaviour of individuals or social groups, and into the 'irrational in politics'. It might also provide mankind with new means of transcending these obstacles.

---

(2). In the words of Thomas Mann (in *'Buddenbrooks'* : 'We are most likely to get angry and excited in our opposition to some idea when we ourselves are not quite certain of our own position, and are inwardly tempted to take the other side'.

The ignored area
and the traditional left

This whole area has been largely ignored by marxist revolutionaries. No blame can be imputed to Marx or Engels for this omission. The appropriate tool for understanding this aspect of human behaviour — namely psychoanalysis — was only developed in the first two decades of this century. Freud's major contributions to knowledge (the investigation of causality in psychological life, the description of infantile and juvenile sexuality, the honest statement of the obvious fact that there was more to sex than procreation, the recognition of the influence of unconscious instinctual drives — and of their repression — in determining behaviour patterns, the description of how such drives are repressed in accordance with the prevailing social dictates, the analysis of the consequences of this repression in terms of symptoms, and in general 'the consideration of the unofficial and unacknowledged sides of human life' [1] only became part of our cultural heritage several decades after Marx's death. Certain reactionary aspects of classical psychoanalysis (the 'necessary' adaptation of the instinctual life to the requirements of a society whose class nature was never explicitly proclaimed, the 'necessary' sublimation of 'undisciplined' sexuality in order to maintain 'social stability', 'civilisation' and the cultural life of society, [2] the theory of the death instinct, etc.) were only to be transcended later still by the revolutionary psychoanalysis of Wilhelm Reich [3] and others.

Reich set out to elaborate a social psychology based on both marxism and psychoanalysis. His aim was to explain how ideas arose in men's minds, in relation to the real condition of their lives, and how in turn such ideas influenced human behaviour. There was clearly a discrepancy between the material conditions of the masses and their conservative outlook. No appeal to psychology was necessary to understand why a hungry man stole bread or why workers, fed up with being pushed around, decided to down tools. What social psychology had to explain however 'is not why the starving individual steals or why the exploited individual strikes, but why the majority of starving individuals do *not* steal, and the majority of exploited individuals do *not* strike'. Classical sociology could 'satisfactory explain a social phenomenon when human thinking and acting serve a rational purpose, when they serve the satisfaction of needs and directly express the economic

---

(1.) B. Malinowski, *'Sex and Repression in Savage Society'* (Merdian Books, Cleveland, 9th printing, November 1966), p. 6.

(2.) An exemple (among many) of Freud's reactionary pronouncements is to be found in his essay *'The Future of an Illusion'*, published in 1927, in which he wrote: 'It is just as impossible to do without control of the mass by a minority as it is to dispense with coercion in the work of civilisation. The masses are lazy and unintelligent : they have no love for instinctual renunciation, and they are not to be convinced by argument of its inevitability ; and the individuals composing them support one another in giving free rein to their indisciple'.

(3.) An excellent study dealing with both Reich, the psychoanalyst, and Reich, the revolutionary, has recently been published in Switzerland (*'La Vie et l'Oeuvre du Docteur Wilhelm Reich'*, by Michel Cattier, La Cité, Lausanne, 1969). It is essential reading for anyone seriously concerned at understanding the tragic life of this remarkable man. The author of this book has borrowed deeply from this source.

situation. It fails, however, when human thinking and acting *contradict* the economic situation, when, in other words, they are irrational'. [4]

What was new, at the level of revolutionary theory, in this kind of concern ? Traditional marxists had always underestimated — and still underestimate — the effect of ideas on the material structure of society. Like parrots, they repeat that economic infrastructures and ideological superstructures mutually interact. But then they proceed to look upon what is essentially a dialectical, two-way relationship as an almost exclusively one-sided process (economic 'base' determining what goes on in the realm of ideas). They have never sought concretely to explain how a reactionary political doctrine could gain a mass foothold and later set a whole nation in motion (how, for instance, in the early 1930s, nazi ideology rapidly spread throughout all layers of German society, the process including the now well-documented massive desertion of thousands of communist militants to the rânks of the Nazis).[5] In the words of a 'herectical' marxist, Daniel Guérin, author of one of the most sophisticated social, economic and psychological interpretations of the fascist phenemenan : 'Some people believe themselves very 'marxist' and very 'materialist' when they neglect human factors and only concern themselves with material and economic facts. They accumulate figures, statistics, percentages. They study with extreme precision the deep causes of social phenomena. But because they don't study with similar precision how these causes are reflected in human consciousness, living reality eludes them. Because they are only interested in material factors, they understand absolutely nothing about how the deprivations endured by the masses are converted into aspirations of a religious type' [6] Neglecting this subjective factor in history, such 'marxists' — and they constitute today the overwhelming majority of the species — cannot explain the lack of correlation between the economic frustrations of the working class and its lack of will to put an end to the system which engenders them. They do not grasp the fact that when certain beliefs become anchored in the thinking (and influence the behaviour) of the masses, they become themselves material facts of history.

(4.) W. Reich *'The Mass Psychology of Fascism'* (Orgone Institute Press, New York, 1946), p. 15.

(5.) No, we are not 'sladering' those courageous German anti-fascists who where among the first to die in Hitler's concentration camps. We are only saying that for every Communist of this kind, at least 2 others joined the Nazis, while dozens of others said nothing and did nothing.

(6.) *'Fascisme et Grand Capital'* (Gallimard, Paris 1945), p. 88.

What was it thereofore, Reich asked, which in the real life of the oppressed limited their will to revolution ? His answer was that the working class was readily influenced by reactionary and irrational ideas because such ideas fell on fertile soil. [7] For the average Marxist, workers were adults who hired their labour power to capitalists and were exploited by them. This was correct as far as it went. But one had to take into account all aspects of working class life if one wanted to undertand the political attitude of the working class. This meant one had to recognise some obvious facts, namely that the worker had a child-hood, that he was brought up by parents themselves conditioned by the society in which they lived, that he had a wife and children, sexual needs, frustrations, and family conflicts. Overcrowding, physical fatigue, financial insecurity, and back-street abortions rendered these problems particularly acute in working class circles. Why should such factors be neglected in seeking to explain working class behaviour ? Reich sought to develop a total analysis which would incorporate such facts and attach the appropriate importance to them.

(7.) In the next section we will describe how the 'soil' is rendered 'fertile' for the acceptance of scch ideas. At this stage we would only like to point out that other sections of the population are also affected. Ruling classes, for instance, are often mystified by their own ideology. But politically this is a phenomenon of lesser signi-ficance ; ruling elites in fact benefit by the maintenance of ideological mystification and of irrational social systems which proclaim the 'need' for such elites!).

The process of
conditioning

In learning to obey their parents children learn obedience in general. The deference learned in the family setting will manifest itself whenever the child faces a 'superior' in later life. Sexual repression — by the already sexually repressed parents [1] — is an integral part of the conditioning process.

Rigid and obsessional parents start by imposing rigid feeding times on the newborn. They then seek to impose regular potting habits on infants scarcely capable of maintaining the sitting posture. They are obsessed by food, bowels, and the 'inculcating of good habits'. A little later they will start scolding and punishing their masturbating 5 year-old. At times they will even threaten their male offspring with physical mutilation. [2] They cannot accept that children at that age — or at any age for that matter — should derive pleasure from sex). They are horrified at their discovery of sexual exhibitionism between consenting juniors in private. Later still they will warn their 12 year-old boys of the dire dangers of 'real masturbation'. They will watch the clock to see at what time their 15 years-old daugthers get home, or search their sons' pockets for contraceptives. For most parents, the child-rearing years are one long, anti-sexual saga.

How does the child react to this ? He adapts by trial and error. He is scolded or punished when he masturbates. He adapts by repressing his sexuality. Attempted reaffirmation of sexual needs then takes the form of a revolt against parental authority. But this revolt is again punished. Obedience is achieved through punishment. Punishment also ensures that forbidden activities are invested with feelings of guilt [3] which may be (but more often aren't) sufficient to inhibit them. [4]

The anxiety associated with the fulfilment of sexual needs becomes part of the anxiety associated with all rebellious thoughts or actions (sexuality and all manifestations of rebelliousness are both indiscriminately curbed by the 'educators'). The child gradually comes to suppress needs whose acting out would incur parental displeasure or result in punishment, and ends up afraid of his sexual drives and of his tendencies to revolt. At a later stage another kind of equilibrium is achieved which has been described as 'being torn between desires that are repugnant to my conscience and a conscience repugnant to my desires'. [5] The individual is 'marked like a road map from head to toes by his repressions'. [6]

(1.) For a discussion of the historical roots of the whole process of sexual repression, see section VI of this book.
(2.) For an extremely amusing account of this kind of conditionning in a New York Jewish family — and of its consequences — see *Portnoy's Complaint* by Philip Roth (Cape, 1968) ... also referred to as The Gripes of Roth.
(3.) Parents are 'the outstanding producers and packagers of guilt in our time'. (P. Roth, op. cit., p. 36).
(4.) This unstable equilibrum is known as 'publicly pleasing my parents while privately my putz'. (ibid., p. 37).
(5.) ibid, p. 132.
(6.) ibid., p. 124.

In the little boy early repression is associated with an identification with the paternal image. In a sense this is a prefiguration of the later identification of the young adult with the 'authority' of 'his' corporation, or with the needs of 'his' country or party. The father, in this sense, is the representative of the state and of authority in the family nucleus.

To neutralise his sexual needs and his rebellion against his parents the child develops 'overcompensations'. The unconscious revolt against the father engenders servility. The fear of sexuality engenders prudery. We all know those old maids of both sexes, ever on the alert against any hint of sexual activity among children. Their preoccupations are obviously determined by deep fears of their own sexuality. The reluctance of most revolutionaries to discuss these topics are similarly motivated.

Another frequent by-product of sexual repression is to split sexuality into its component parts. Tenderness is given a positive value whereas sensuality is condemned. A dissociation between affection and sexual pleasure is seen in many male adolescents and leads them to adopt double sexual standards. They idealise some girl on a pedestal while seeking to satisfy their sexual needs with other girls whom they openly or subconsciously despise.

The road to a healthy sex life for adolescents is blocked by both external and internal obstacles. The external obstacles (difficulty in finding an undisturbed place, difficulty in escaping from family surveillance, etc.) are obvious enough. The internal (psychological) obstacles may at times be severe enough to influence the perception of the sexual need. The two kinds of obstacles (internal and external) mutually reinforce one another. External factors consolidate sexual repression and the sexual repression predisposes to the influence of the external factors. The family is the hub of this vicious circle.

However apparently successful the repression, the repressed material is of course still there. But it is now running in subterranean channels. Having accepted a given set of 'cultural' values, the individual must now defend himself against anything that might disrupt the painfully established equilibrium. He has constantly to mobilise part of his psychological potentialities against the 'disturbing' influences. In addition to neuroses and psychoses the 'energy' expended in this constant repression results in difficulties in thought and concentration, in a diminution of awareness and probably in some impairment of mental capacity. 'Inability to concentrate' is perhaps the most common of all neurotic symptoms.

According to Reich, the "suppression of the natural sexuality in the child, particularly of its genital sexuality, makes the child apprehensive, shy, obedient, afraid of authority, 'good' and 'adjusted' in the authoritarian sense ; it paralyzes the rebellious forces because any rebellion is laden with anxiety ; it produces, by inhibiting sexual curiosity and sexual thinking in the child, a general inhibition of thinking and of critical faculties. In brief the goal of sexual repression is that of producing an individual who is adjusted to the authoritarian order and who will submit to it in spite of all misery and degradation. . . . The result is fear of freedom, and a conservative, reactionary mentality. *Sexual repression aids political reaction, not only through this process which makes the mass individual passive and unpolitical, but also by creating in his structure an interest in actively supporting the authoritarian order".* [7] My emphasis — M.B.)

When the child's upbringing has been completed the individual has acquired something more complex and harmful than a simple obedience response to those in authority. He has developed a whole system of reactions, repressions, thoughts, rationalisations, which form a character structure adepted to the authoritarian social system. The purpose of education — both East and West — is the mass production of robots of this kind who have so internalised social constraints that they submit to them automatically.

Psychologists and psychiatrists have written pages about the *medical* effects of sexual repression. [8] Reich however constantly reiterated its *social* function, exercised through the family. The purpose of sexual repression was to anchor submission to authority and the fear of freedom into peoples' 'character armour'. The net result was the reproduction, generation after generation, of the basic conditions essential for the manipulation and enslavement of the masses.

(7.) W. Reich *'The Mass Psychology of Fascism'* pp. 25-26.
(8.) This factual approach is a relatively recent development. As Kinsey, Pomeroy and Martin point out their famous study on the *'Sexual Behaviour of the Human Male'* (Saunders, Philadelphia 1948, pp. 21-22) : 'From the dawn of human history, from the drawings left by primitive peoples, on through the developments of all civilisations (ancient, classic oriental medieval and modern), men have recorded their sexual activities and their thinking about sex. The printed literature is enormous and the other material is inexhaustible . . . (This literature) is at once an interesting reflection on man's absorbing interest in sex and his astounding ignorance of it ; his desire to know and his unwillingness to face the facts ; his respect for an objective scientific approach to the problems involved and his overwhelming urge to be poetic, pornographic, literary, philosophic, traditional and moral . . . in short to do anything except ascertain the basic facts about himself'.

The function of the family

In his classical study on '*The Origin of the Family, Private Property and the State*', Engels attributes three main functions to the family in capitalist society :

It was *a mechanism for the transmission of wealth through inheritance,* a process which permitted the dominant social groups to perpetuate their economic power. This has undoubtedly been an important function of the bourgeois family. However Engels' hope that 'with the disappearance of private property the family would lose its last reason to exist' has not materialised. The private ownership of the means of production has been abolished in Russia for over 50 years and yet the family (in the compulsive, bourgeois sense) still seems deeply embedded both in Russian consciousness and in Russian reality. By a strange paradox, it is in the capitalist West that the bourgeois family is being submitted to the most radical critique — in both theory and practice.

The family was also *a unit of economic production,* particularly in the countryside and in petty trade. Large-scale industry and the general drift to the towns characteristic of the 20th century have markedly reduced the significance of this function.

The family was finally *a mechanism for the propagation of the human species.* This statement is also correct, in relation to a whole period of human history. It should not of course be taken to imply that, were it not for the civil or religious marriages of the bourgeois type (what Engels called those 'permits to practice sex'), the propagation of the human species would abruptly cease ! Other types of relationships (more or less lasting, monogamous — or otherwise — while they last) are certainly conceivable. In a communist society technological changes and new living patterns would largely do away with household chores. The bringing up of children would probably not be the exclusive function of one pair of individuals for more than a short time. What are usually given as psychological reasons for the perpetuation of the compulsive marriage are often just rationalisations.

Engels' comments about the family, partly valid as they still are (and valid as they have been) don't really allow one to grasp the full significance of this institution. They ignore a whole dimension of life. Classical psychoanalysis hinted at a further function : the transmission of the dominant cultural pattern. Revolutionary psychoanalysis was to take this concept much further.

Freud himself had pointed out that parents brought up their children according to the dictates of their own (the parents') superegos. [1] 'In general parents and similar authorities follow

(1.) According to the Freudian model the personality consists of the id, the ego, and the super-ego. The first and last are unconscious. The id is the sum total of the instinctual drives of the individual. The super-ego is a kind of internal policeman, originating in the constraints exercised on the individual 'on behalf of society' by parents and other educators. The *ego* is man's conscious self.

the dictates of their own super-egos in the upbringing of children . . . In the education of the child they are severe and exacting. They have forgotten the difficulties of their own childhood, and are glad to be able to identify themselves fully at last with their own parents, who in their day subjected them to such severe restraints. The result is that the super-ego of the child is not really built upon the model of the parents but on that of the parents' super-ego. It takes over the same content, it becomes the vehicle of tradition and of all the age-long values which have been handed down in this way from generation to generation . . . Mankind never lives completely in the present ; the ideologies of the super-ego perpetuate the past, the traditions of the race and the people, which yield but slowly to the influence of the present and to new developments. So long as they work through the super-ego, they play an important part in man's life, quite independently of economic conditions'. [2]

Reich was to develop these ideas to explain the lag between class consciousness and economic reality, and the tremendous social inertia represented by habits of deference and submission among the oppressed. In order to do this he had to launch a frontal assault on the institution of the bourgeois family. an assault which was to provoke heated attacks upon him. These were to be launched not only by reactionaries and religious bigots of all kinds, but also by orthodox psychoanalysts [3] and by orthodox Marxists. [4]

'As the economic basis (of the family) became less significant', Reich wrote, 'its place was taken by the political function which the family now began to assume. Its cardinal function, that for which it is mostly supported and defended by conservative science and law, is that of serving as *a factory for authoritarian ideologies and conservative structures*. It forms the educational apparatus through which practically every individual of our society, from the moment of drawing his first breath, has to pass . . . *it is the conveyor belt between the econo-*

(2.) S. Freud. *'New Introductory Lectures on Psychoanalysis'* (The Hogarth Press, London 1933, pp. 90-91.).

(3.) In 1927 Freud himself warned Reich, his former pupil, that in attacking the family he was 'walking into a hornet's nest'. In August 1934 Reich was to be expelled from the German Association of Psychoanalysts.

(4.) Reich was expelled from the German Communist Party in 1933. In December 1932 the Party had forbidden the circulation of his works in the Communist Youth Movement, among whom they had evoked a considerable echo. Marxist and psychoanalyst, Reich saw his work condemned by those who claimed to be the standard-bearers of marxism and of psychoanalysis. A little later the Nazis were also to forbid the circulation of his works in Germany.

mic structure of conservative society and its ideological super-structure'. [5]

Reich probed ruthlessly into familial behaviour. The pre-dominating type (the 'lower middle class' family) extended high up the social scale, but even further down into the class of industrial workers. Its basis was 'the relation of the patriar-chal father to his wife and children ... because of the contra-diction between his position in the productive process (subor-dinate) and his family function (boss) he is sergeant-major type. He kowtows to those above, absorbs the prevailing attitudes (hence his tendency to imitation) and dominates those below. He transmits the governmental and social concepts and enforces them'. [6] The process is 'mitigated in the industrial workers' milieu by the fact that the children are much less supervised'. [7]

Nearly all reactionaries clearly perceive that sexual freedom would subvert the compulsive marriage and with it the authori-tarian structure of which the family is a part. (The attitude of the Greek colonels during the recent dictatorship, towards miniskirts, co-education and 'permissive' literature would be a textbook example of what we are talking about.) Sexual inhi-bitions must therefore be anchored in the young. 'Authoritarian society is not concerned about 'morality per se'. Rather, the anchoring of sexual morality and the changes it brings about in the organism create that specific psychic structure which forms the mass-psychological basis of any authoritarian social order. The vassal-structure is a mixture of sexual impotence, helplessness, longing for a Fuhrer, fear of authority, fear of life, and mysticism. It is characterised by devout loyalty and simultaneous rebellion ... People with such a structure are inca-pable of democratic living. Their structure nullifies all attempts at establishing or maintaining organisations run along truly democratic principles. [8] They form the mass-psychological soil on which the dictatorial or bureaucratic tendencies of their de-mocratically-elected leaders can develop'. [9]

A class society can only function as long as those it exploits accept their exploitation. The statement would seem so obvious as hardly to need elaboration. Yet there are, on the political scene today, groups who maintain that the conditions are 'rotten ripe

(5.) W. Reich *'The Sexual Revolution'* (The Noonday Press, New York 1962), p. 72.
(6.) Ibid., p. 73.
(7.) Ibid., p. 75.
(8.) The relevance of this to most 'left' organisations hardly needs stressing. The revolutionaries themselves — in this as in so many other respects — are among the worst enemies of the revolution.
(9.) Ibid., p. 79.

for revolution' and that only the lack of an appropriate leadership prevents the revolutionary masses, yearning for a total transformation of their conditions of life, from carrying out such a revolution. Unfortunately this is very far from being the case. In an empirical way even Lenin perceived this. In April 1917 he wrote : 'The bourgeoisie maintains itself not only by force but also by the lack of consciousness, by the force of custom and habit among the masses'. [10]

It is obvious that if large sections of the population were constantly questioning the principles of hierarchy, the authoritarian organisation of production, the wages system, or other fundamental aspects of the social structure, no ruling class could maintain itself in power for long. For rulers to continue ruling it is necessary that those at the bottom of the social ladder not only accept their condition but eventually lose even the sense of being exploited. Once this psychological process has been achieved the division of society becomes legitimised in people 's minds. The exploited cease to perceive it as something imposed on them from without. The oppressed have internalised their own oppression. They tend to behave like robots, programmed not to rebel against the established order. The robots may even seek to defend their subordinate position, to rationalise it and will often reject as 'pie-in-the-sky' any talk of emancipation. They are often impermeable to progressive ideas. Only at times of occasional insurrectionary outbursts do the rulers have to resort to force, as a kind of reinforcement of a conditioning stimulus.

Reich describes this process as follows : 'It is not merely a matter of imposing ideologies, attitudes and concepts on the members of society. It is a matter of a deep-reaching process in each new generation of the formation of a psychic structure which corresponds to the existing social order, in all strata of the population ... Because this order moulds the psychic structure of all members of society it reproduces itself in people ... *the first and most important place of reproduction of the social order is the patriarchal family* which creates in children a character structure which makes them amenable to the later influence of an authoritarian order ... this characteriological anchoring of the social order explains the tolerance of the

---

(10.) V.I. Lenin. *'Selected Works'*, vol. VI, p. 36. Lenin wrote this despite a complete lack of understanding or awareness of the mechanism whereby 'the force of custom and habit among the masses' were mediated and perpetuated. This lack of understanding was to lead to his open hostility to the sexual revolution which swept Russia in the wake of the Civil War and to contribute yet another element to the bureaucratic degeneration.

It is impossible to understand how or why sexual repression originated — and what influences maintain, enhance or weaken it — without seeing the problem in a much wider context, namely that of the historical evolution of relations between the sexes, in particular of the evolution of such human relationships as kinship and marriage. These are the central concerns of modern social anthropology.

The whole subject is like a minefield, littered with methodological and terminological trip wires. About a hundred years ago a number of important books were published which shook established thinking to the roots, in that they questioned the immutability of human institutions and behaviours. [1] The authors of these books played an important role in the history of anthropology. They sought to put the subject on a firm historical basis. They pointed out important connections between forms of marriage and sexual customs on the one hand and — on the other hand — such factors as the level of technology, the inheritance of property, and the authority relations prevailing within various social groups, etc. They founded the whole study of kinship and gave it its terminology. But carried away in the great scientific and ratonalist euphoria of the late 19th century these authors generalised far beyond what was permissible on the basis of the available data. They constructed great schemes and drew conclusions about the history of mankind which some modern experts have politely described as 'famous pseudo-historical speculations' [2] and other as 'quite staggeringly without foundation'. [3]

We will now briefly summarise these 'classical' conceptions (in relation to the areas which concern us) with a view to commenting on what is still valid within them, what is dubious and what can no longer be accepted in the light of modern knowledge.

In primitive societies the level of technology was very low and there was no surplus product to be appropriated by non-productive sections of the community. There was an elementary, 'biological' division of labour : the men who were strongest,

(1.) Among such books one should mention J.J. Bachofen's *Das Mutterrecht* Stuttgart, 1861), J. F. McLennan's *Primitive Marriage* (Black, London, 1876), L. H. Morgan's *Ancient Society* (Holt, New York 1870) and *Systems of Consanguinity and Affinity of the Human Family* (Smithsonian Institute, Washington 1877), Engel's *The Origin of the Family, Private Property and the State* (Zurich 1884), and E. Westermarck's *The History of Human Marriage* (Macmillan, London 1889).

(2.) See A. R. Radcliffe-Brown and D. Forde's *African Systems of Kinship and Marriage*, O.U.P. 1950, p. 72.

(3.) R. Fox, *Kinship and Marriage* Penguin Books, 1967, p. 18.

went out hunting or sowed the fields ; the women prepared the meals and looked after the children. It was held that in these societies 'group marriages' were common. As result it was difficult or impossible to know the father of any particular child. The mother, of course, was always known and descent was therefore acknowledged in matrilinear terms. Such societies were described as 'matriarchal'. With improvements in technology (the discovery of bronze and copper, the smelting of iron ore, the manufacture of implements, the development of new methods of soil cultivation and of rearing cattle) it soon became possible for two arms to produce more than one mouth could consume. War and the capture of slaves became a meaningful proposition. The economic role of the men in the tribe soon assumed a preponderance which was no longer in keeping with their equivocal social status. In Engels' words 'as wealth increased it on the one hand gave the man a more important status in the family than the woman, and on the other hand it created a stimulus to utilise this strengthened position to overthrow the traditional order of inheritance in favour of his children. But this was impossible as long as descent according to mother-right prevailed'. [4]

According to the classical theory a profound change then took place, probably spread over many centuries, which Engels described as the world historic defeat of the female sex. [5] The male gradually became the dominant sex, both economically and socially. Women became a commodity to be exchanged against cattle or weapons. With further changes in the productivity of labour, a definite social surplus was now being produced. Those who had access to this surplus sought to institutionalise their right to it os private property and to leave part of it to their descendants. But to do this they had to know who their descendants were. Hence the appearance of the patriarchal family, of monogamous marriage, and of a sexual morality which stressed female chastity and which demanded of women virginity before marriage and faithfulness during it. Female unfaithfulness becomes a crime punishable by death for it allows doubts to arise as to the legitimacy of the descendants.

(4) F. Engels *The Origin of the Family, Private Property and the State*. Foreign Language Publishing House, Moscow 1954, p. 92.
(5) Ibid., p. 94.

What is false in this schema is the notion — often explicitly stated — that the whole of mankind went through a series stages characterised by specific forms of social organisation and specific patterns of inheritance.

There is little evidence that societies based on 'matriarchy' [6] or even on 'mother-right' were ever universally dominant forms. It is wrong to regard any contemporary tribe in which matrilinear descent still pertains as some kind of fossil, arrested at an earlier stage of evolutionary development. [7] It is also wrong to associate specific marriage forms with specific level of technological development ('group marriage' for 'savage society', 'the syndiasmic family' for 'barbarism', 'monogamous marriage' for 'civilisation', etc.) This is not to say that kinship systems are arbitrary. They are adaptable and have certainly been adapted to fulfil varying human needs. These 'needs' have differed widely according to population density, climatic conditions, land fertility, and numerous other variables, known and unknown. The alternatives 'patriarchal' — 'matriarchal' are moreover extremely naive. [8] We now know that we must distinguish between matrilinear, patrilinear or 'cognatic' (kinship through both lines) patterns of inheritance and between matrilocal and patrilocal (who lives where?) patterns of abode, and that these in turn exercise considerable influence on social and sexual mores. There are also differences between person-to-person relationships and obligations (inheritance, etc.) and group obligations (in relation to common or impartible land, to ancestor worship, to 'duties' to avenge death, etc.) and these may conflict. Reality

---

(6) There has probably never been a truly 'matriarchal' society in the sense of a mirror-image of patriarchal society. The notion of such a society where wives hold the purse strings, order their husbands about, beat them up from time to time and take all the important decisions concerning both individuals and the tribe as whole is at best a retrospective projection or nightmare of guilt-laden males.

(7) It is interesting that the best known modern matrilinear societies (the Nayars of Kerala and the Menangkabau Malays) far from being 'primitive' are advanced, literate and cultured people, who have produced an extensive literature. The Khasi of Assam are less advanced but are far from being savages. As Radcliffe-Brown and Forde point out (*African Systems of Kinship and Marriage*): 'the typical instances of mother-right are found not amongst the most primitive people but in advanced or relatively advanced societies'.

(8) In this they resemble many of the 'alternatives' propounded today by so-called revolutionaries (for instance 'monogamous marriage' or 'communes' for life 'after the Revolution').

is extremely complex in its manifestations and these cannot today be as readily 'tidied up' as they were in the past. Moreover the 'very rigidity of the (classical) theories makes them difficult to use and is in stark contrast to the malleability of human beings'. [9]

What remains therefore of the classical schema ? Firstly the intellectual courage and ambition of seeking to grasp reality in its totality and of not seeking refuge behind the complexity of facts to proclaim the incoherance of nature. When one hears that 'modern anthropology' has 'invalidated Morgan' one is reminded of oft heard verdicts that 'modern sociology' has 'invalidated Marx'. At one level this is true but there is also a deliberately entertained confusion between perspective and detail, between method and content, between intention and fulfilment.

At the more specific level it remains true that the appearance of a social surplus led to a struggle for its appropriation and to attempts to restrict its dispersal by institutionalised means. It is also true that by and large this process was associated with a progressive restriction of female sexual rights and with the 'patriarchal' functions the more repressive the societies have some matrilinear societies may have been sexually inhibited, and although not all patriarchal societies are necessarily repressive, it remains true that by and large the more widespread the 'patriarchal' functions the more repressive the societies have been. Modern psychoanalysis may throw further light on the mechanisms whereby this came about. At this stage we can only pinpoint an area that badly needs to be studied.

The 'inferior' status of women soon came to be widely accepted. Over the centuries, throughout slave society, feudal society and capitalist society — but also in the many parts of the world which have *not* gone through this sequence — a whole ethos, a whole philosophy and whole set of social customs were to emerge which consecrated this subordinate relationship, both in real life and in the minds of both men and women.

The sacred texts of the Hindus limit women's access to freedom and to material belongings. The Ancient Greeks were profoundly misogynist and relegated their women to the gynecaeum. Pythagoras speaks of 'a good principle which created order, light and man — and a bad principle which created chaos, darkness and woman'. Demonsthenes proclaimed that 'one took a wife to have legitimate children, concubines to

---

(9) P. Fox. op. cit. p. 63.

be well looked after and courtesans for the pleasures of physical love'. Plato in his *Republic* declares that 'the most holy marriages are those which are of most benefit to the State'. The fathers of the Christian Church soon succeed in destroying the early hopes of freedom and emancipation which led many women to martyrdom. Women become synonymous with eternal temptation. They are seen as a constant 'invitation to fornication, a trap for the unwary'. Saint Paul states that 'man was not created for woman, but woman for man'. Saint John Chrysostome proclaims that 'among all wild beasts, none are as dangerous as women'. According to St. Thomas Aquinas 'woman is destined to live under man's domination and has no authority of her own right'.

These attitudes were perpetuated in the dominant ideology of the Middle Ages and even into more recent times. Milton, in *Paradis Lost,* proclaims that 'man was made for God and woman was made for man'. Schopenhauser defines woman as 'an animal with long hair and short ideas', Nietzche calls her 'the warrior's pastime'. Even the muddle-headed Proudhon sees her as 'housewife or courtesan' and proclaims that 'neither by nature or destiny can woman be an associate, a citizen or a holder of public office'. Kaiser Wilhelm the Second defined a role for women (later echoed by the Third Reich) as being 'Kirche, Küche, Kinder' (Church, Kitchen and Kids).

In 1935 Wilhelm Reich wrote a major *'Der Einbruch der Sexual-moral* which discusses how an authoritarian sexual morality developed. The book has not been translated into English and copies of it are very difficult to find. In it Reich discusses some interesting observations of Malinowski's concerning the inhabitants of the Trobriand Islands (off Eastern New Guinea), where matrilinear forms of kinship prevailed. (Reich had met Malinowski in London in 1934.) Among the Trobrianders there was free sexual play during childhood and considerable sexual freedom during adolescence. Tics and neuroses were virtually unknown and the general attitude to life was easy and relaxed. Reich discusses however the practice whereby, among the ruling groups, certain girls were encouraged to marry their first cousins (the sons of the mother's brother) thereby enabling marriage settlements to be recuperated and to remain within the family. Whereas sexual freedom was widespread among all other young Trobrianders, those destined for a marriage of this kind were submitted from an early age to all sorts of sexual taboos. Economic interests — the accumulation of wealth within the ruling group — determined restrictions of sexual freedom within this group.

Reich vividly contrasts the Trobrianders and other sexually unihibited societies with classical patriarchal societies which produce mass neurosis and mass misery through sexual repression. With the strengthening of patriarchy the family acquires, in addition to its economic function, the far more significant function of changing the human structure from that of the free clan member to that of the suppressed family member ... the relationship between clan members, which was free and voluntary, based only on common vital interests, is replaced by a conflict between economic and sexual interests. Voluntary achievement in work replaced by compulsive work and rebellion against it. Natural sexual sociality is replaced by the demands of morality ; voluntary, happy love relationship is replaced by « marital duty » ; clan solidarity is replaced by familial ties and rebellion against them ; sex-economically regulated life is replaced by genital repression, neurotic disturbances and sexual perversions ; the naturally stronge, self-reliant biological organism become weak, helpless, dependent, fearful of God ; the orgasic experiencing of nature is replaced by mystical ecstasy, « religious experience » and unfulfilled vegetative longing ; the weakened ego of the individual seeks strength in the identification with the tribe, later the « nation » , and with the chief of the tribe, later the patriarche of the tribe and the king of the nation. [10] With that the birth of the vassal structure has taken place ; the structural anchoring of human subjugation is secured.' [11]

(10) Or with the Party — or the General Secretary of the Party — whoever he may momentarily be. — M.B.
(11) W. Reich. 'The Sexual Revolution' pp. 161-162.

Wilhelm Reich and the sexual revolution

Those who want to change society must seek to under-stand how people act and think in society. This is not a field in which traditional revolutionaries are at home. For reasons we have shown they feel distinctly uncomfortable in it. Reich's views on social conditioning are certainly of relevance here, whatever one may think of other aspects of his work. [1]

Some possible misunderstandings should be cleared up immediately. We are not saying that the sexual revolution is *the* revolution. We have not abandoned the fight for the Revolution to become 'prophets of the better orgasm'. We are not in transit from collective revolutionary politics to individual sexual emancipation. We are not saying that sexual factors are to be *substituted* for economic ones in the understanding of social reality or that understanding sexual repression will automatically generate an insight into the mechanisms of exploitation and alienation which are at the root of class society. Nor are we endorsing Reich's later writings, whether in the field of biology or in the field of politics.

What we *are* saying is that revolution is a total phenomenon or it is nothing, [2] that a social revolution which is not *also* a sexual revolution is unlikely to have gone much below the surface of things, and that sexual emancipation is not something that will 'come later', 'automatically' or as a 'by-product' of a revolution in other aspects of people's lives. We are stressing that no 'understanding' of social reality can be total which neglects the sexual factors and that sexual repression itself has both economic origins and social effects. We are trying to explain some of the difficulties confronting revolutionaries and some of the real problems they are up against — here and now. We are finally trying to explain why the task of the purely 'industrial' militant or of the purely 'political' revolutionary is so diffucult, unrewarding and in the long run sterile.

Unless revolutionaries are clearly aware of *all* the resistances they are up against, how can they hope to break them down ? Unless revolutionaries are aware of the resistances (i.e. the unsuspected influences of the dominant ideology) within themselves, how can they hope to get to grips with problems of others ?

How much of the life of the ordinary person is devoted to 'politics' (even in basic terms of organised economic struggle) and how much to problems of interpersonal relationships ? To ask the question is already to provide an answer. Yet just look at the average left political literature today. Reading the columns

---

(1.) In the last years of his life Reich developed paranoid symptoms and quarrelled with nearly all his erstwhile supporters. He was driven mad, at least in part, by the apparently insoluble contradiction 'no social revolution without sexual revolution — no sexual revolution without social revolution'. A recent biography *'Wilhelm Reich'* by Ilse Ollendorf Reich (Elek, London 1969), his third wife, gives a fairly objective account of the last phase of the life of this remarkable man.

(2.) As St. Just once emphasised, 'those who will only carry out half a revolution dig their own graves' .

of the *Morning Star, Workers' Press, Militant, Socialist Worker or Socialist Standard,* one doesn't get a hint that the problems discussed in this book even exist. Man is seen as a ridiculous fragment of his full stature. One seldom gets the impression that the traditional revolutionaries are talking about real people, whose problems in relation to wives, parents, companions or children occupy at least as much of their lives as their struggle against economic exploitation. Marxists sometimes state (but more often just imply) that a change in the property relations (or in the relations of production) will initiate a process which will eventually solve the emotional problems of mankind (an end to sexual misery through a change in the leaderships ?). This does not follow in the least. If Marx is right, that 'socialism is man's positive self-consciousness', the struggle at the level of sexual emancipation must be waged in explicit terms and victory not just left to happen (or not happen) in the wake of economic change. It is difficult however to convince the average revolutionary of this. Their own 'character armour' renders them impervious to the basic needs of many of those on whose behalf they believe they are acting. They are afraid to politicise the sexual question because they are afraid of what is in themselves.

What are the practical implications of the ideas we have here outlined ? Can the sexual revolution take place within a capitalist context ? Can a total revolution take place while people are still sexually repressed ? We hope in this section to show that even posing the question in these terms is wrong and that there is a profound dialectical relation between the two which should never be lost sight of.

Reich originally hoped it might be possible to eliminate people's neuroses by education, explanation and a change in their sexual habits. But he soon came to realise that it was a waste of time to line patients up for the analyst's couch if society was producing neuroses faster than analysts were capable of coping with them. Capitalist society was a mass production industry as far as neuroses were concerned. And where it did not produce well-defined, clinically recognisable neuroses, it often produced 'adaptations' that crippled the individual by compelling him to submit. (In modern society submission and adaptation are often the price paid for avoiding an individual neurosis.) Growing awareness of this fact led Reich increasingly to question the whole pattern of social organisation and to draw revolutionary conclusions. He came to see that 'the sexual problem' was deeply related to authoritarian social structures and could not be solved short of overthrowing the established order.

At this point many would have abandoned psychoanalysis for radical politics of the classical type. What makes Reich such an interesting and original thinker is that he also perceived the converse, namely that it would be impossible fundamentally to alter the existing social order as long as people were conditioned (through sexual repression and an authoritarian upbringing) into accepting the fundamental norms of the society around them. Reich joined the Austrian Communist Party in July 1927 following the shootings in Schattendorf and Vienna.[3] He participated in meetings, leafleting, demonstrations, etc. But he simultaneously continued to develop revolutionary psychoanalysis, guiding it into biologically uncharted territory. He took it from where it ceased to be a comfortable profession into areas where it began to be a dangerous occupation. He set up free sexual hygiene clinics in the working class districts of Vienna. These proved extremely popular. They gave Reich a very deep insight not only into the sexual and economic misery of the population, but also into 'the acquired irrational structure of the masses' which made 'dictatorship through utilisation of the irrational possible'.[4] In Reich's writings 'man' as patient and man' very social being merged more and more into one. Reich's very experiences in politics (the endorsement and 'justification' of police brutality by large sections of the Austrian population, the acceptance of authority even by the starving, the relatively easy accession to power by the Nazis in Germany, the triumph of the 'political pirates' over the 'repressed and hungry masses') led him to question ever more deeply the mechanisms whereby the dominant ideology permeated the ranks of oppressed, to search ever more thoroughly for the roots of the 'irrational in politics'.

Reich's conclusions have already been indicated : people's character structure prevents them from becoming aware of their real interests. The fear of freedom, the longing for order (of *any* kind), the panic at the thought of being deprived of a

---

(3.) Early in 1927, in the little Austrian town of Schattendorf, some members of the Heimwehr (a paramilitary, right-wing formation, part of which later defected to the Nazis) had opened fire from a barricaded inn on a peaceful procession of Socialist workers, killing 2 and wounding many. On July 14 the assassins were acquitted by a judge faithful to the Old Regime. The following day there was a mass strike and street demonstrations in Vienna, in the course of which the crowd set fire to the Palace of 'Justice'. The police opened fire at short range. 85 civilians, all workers, were killed, some of them by police whom they were actually trying to rescue from the burning building. Most of the dead were buried in a mass 'Grave of Honour' provided by the Vienna Council, then under Socialist control. The events proved a turning point in Austrian history. For further details see *'Fallen Bastions'*, by G.E.R.Geyde.

(4.) W. Reich. *'The Mass Psychology of Fascisc'*, p. 212.

leader, the anxiety with which they confront pleasure or new ideas, the distress caused by having to think for oneself, all act against any wish at social emancipation. 'Now we understand', Reich wrote 'a basic element in the "retroaction of ideology on the economic base". Sexual inhibition alters the structure of the economically suppressed individual in such a manner that he think, feels and acts against his own material interests'.[5]

It might be thought that only pessimistic conclusions could flow from such an analysis. If a rational attitude to sexuality is impossible under capitalism (because the continuation of capitalism precludes the development of rationality in general), and if no real social change is possible as long as people are sexually repressed (because this conditions their acceptance of authority) the outlook would seem bleak indeed, in relation to both sexual and social revolutions.

Cattier's biography of Reich contains a passage which brilliantly illustrates this dilemma : 'When Reich was with his patients he had noticed that they would mobilise all their defence reactions against him. They would hang on to their neurotic equilibrium and experience fear as the analyst got near the repressed material. In the same way revolutionary ideas slither off the character armour of the masses because such ideas are appealing to everything that people had had to smother within themsleves in order to put up with their own brutalisation.

'It would be wrong to believe that working people fail to revolt because they lack information about the mechanisms of economic exploitation. In fact revolutionary propoganda which seeks to explain to the masses the social injustice and irrationality of the economic system falls on deaf ears. Those who get up at 5 in the morning to work in a factory, and have on top of it to spend 2 hours of every day on underground or suburban trains have to adapt to these conditions by eliminating from their mind anything that might put such conditions in question again. If they realised that they were wasting their lives in the service of an absurd system they would either go mad or commit suicide. To avoid achieving such anxiety-laden insight they justify their existence by rationalising it.[6] They repress anything that might disturb them and acquire a character structure adapted to the conditions under which they must live. Hence it follows that the idealistic tactic consisting of explaining to people that

---

(5.) See footnote 3, page.

(6.) This absolutely correct. It is often the most oppressed economically and the most culturally deprived who will argue most strenuously about the need for leaders and hierarchy and about the impossibility of equality or workers' management, all of which are vehemently described as contrary to 'human nature'. — M.B.

they are oppressed is useless, as people have had to suppress the perception of oppression in order to live with it. Revolutionary propagandists often claim they are trying to raise people's level of consciousness. Experience shows that their endeavours are seldom successful. Why ? Because such endeavours come up against all the unconscious defence mechanisms and against all the various rationalisations that people have built up in order *not to* become aware of the exploitation and of the void in their lives.

This sombre image has far more truth in it than most revolutionaries can comfortably admit. But in the last analysis it is inadequate. It is inadequate because it implies *totally* malleable individuals, in whom *total* sexual repression has produced the prerequisites for *total* conditioning and therefore for *total* acceptance of the dominant ideology. The image is inadequate because it is undialectical. It does not encompass the possibility that attitudes might change, that the 'laws' governing psychological mechanisms might alter, that a fight against sexual repression (dictated by sexual needs themselves) might loosen the 'character armour' of individuals and render them more capable of rational thought and action. In a sense the model described implies a vision of psychological reactions as something unalterable and fixed, governed by objective laws which operate independently of the actions or wishes of men. In this sense it bears a strange similarity to the image of capitalism present in the it bears a strange similarity to the image of capitalism present mind of so many revolutionaries. [7] But neither the external nor the internal world of man in fact exist in this form. The working class does not submit to its history, until one day it makes it explode. Its continuous struggle in production constantly modifies the arena on which the next phase of the struggle will have to be fought. The working class itself is change in the process. Much the same applies to man's struggle for sexual freedom.

Reich himself was aware of this possibility. In the preface the first edition of 'Character Analysis' (1933) he wrote : 'Gradually, with the development of the social process, there develops an increasing discrepancy between enforced renunciation and increased libidinal tension : *this discrepancy undermines 'tradition' and forms the psychological core of attitudes which theaten the anchoring'.*

(7.) See *'Modern Capitalism and Revolution'* by Paul Cardan (in particular the chapter on 'Capitalist ideology yesterday and today'). Obtainable from OUR GENERATION, 3934 St. Urbain St. Montréal, Canada.

Limits and perspectives

The 'undermining of tradition' to which Reich referred has certainly progressed within recent years. The change in traditional attitudes is both gaining momentum and becoming more explicit in a manner which would have surprised and delighted Reich. Seeing the havoc around him in the working class districts of Vienna and Berlin (in the late 1920s and early 1930s) Reich wrote brilliant and bitter pages about the sexual misery of adolescence, about the damage done to the personality by guilt about masturbation, about ignorance and misinformation concerning birth control, about the high cost of contraceptives, about back street abortions (so often the fate of the working class girl or housewife) and about the hypocrisy of the 'compulsive' bourgeois marriage with its inevitable concomitant of young, Reich wrote, would mean the end of this type of marriage. jealousy, adultery and prostitution. Real sexual freedom for the Bourgeois society needed bourgeois marriage as one of the corner stones of its edifice. For Reich any large scale sexual freedom was inconceivable within the framework of capitalism.

What has happened has been rather different from anything Reich could have foreseen. In advanced industrial societies the persistent struggle of the young for what is one of their fundamental rights — the right to a normal sex life from the age at which they are capable of it — has succeeded in denting the repressive ideology, in bringing about changes and in modifying the ground on which the next stage of the struggle will have to be fought. Adolescents are breaking out of the stifling atmosphere of the traditional family, an act which could be of considerable significance. Information and practical help about birth control is now available, even to the non-married. The increasing financial independance of young people and the discovery of oral contraception provide a solid material foundation for the whole process. The attitude to 'illegitimacy' is gradually changing. The upbringing of children is more enlightened. Abortion is now more widely available, divorce much easier and the economic rights of women more widely recognised. Understanding, is increasing. People are beginning to grasp that society itself engenders the anti-social behaviour which it condemns. It is true that all this has only been achieved on a small scale, only in some countries[1] and anly it the face of tremendous opposition. It is also true that, as in Reich's day, every concession is 'too late and too little', belatedly recognising established facts rather than blazing a new trail. Moreover none of the 'reformers' are as yet demystified or unrepressed enough boldly to trumpet the message that sex is a natural and pleasurable activity — or that the right to sexual happiness is a basic human right. It is rarely proclaimed that throughout history the practice of sex has never had procreation as its main end, whatever the preachings of moralists, priests, philosophers or politicians. But despite these limitations the fact of a developing sexual revolution is undeniable, irreversible and of deep significance.

As in other areas, the attempt at sexual emancipation encounters two kinds of response from established society : frontal opposition — from those who still live in the Victorian era — and an attempt at recuperation. Modern society seeks first to neuralise any threat presented to it, and ultimately to convert such challenges into something useful to its own ends.

(1.) In Catholic or Muslim countries, sexual repression remains a pillar of the social order. But even the Catholic Church is having trouble (both with its clergy and with its youth). And among the Palestinian guerillas women are fighting alongside men. This fight cannot be waged wearing a yasmak or accepting traditional Arab values as to the role and function of women in society.

It seeks to regain with one hand what it has been compelled to yield with the other : parts of its control of the total situation.

In relation to sex, the phenomenon of recuperation takes the form of first alienating and reifying sexuality, and then of frenetically exploiting this empty shell for commercial ends. As modern youth breaks out of the dual stranglehold of repressive traditional morality and of the authoritarian patriarchal family it encounters a projected image of free sexuality which is in fact a manipulatory distortion of it. The image is often little more than a means of selling products. Today sex is used to sell everything from cigarettes to real estate, from bottles of perfume to pay-as-you-earn holidays, from hair lotions to models of next year's car. The potential market is systematically surveyed, quantitated, exploited. The 'pornographic' explosion on Broad Street (New York) now caters to a previously repressed clientele of massive proportions and varied tastes. Here as elsewhere it is often a question of consumer research. Separate booths and displays are arranged for homosexual (active and passive), for fetishists, for sadists, for masochists, for voyeurs, etc. Fashion advertising, strip-tease shows and certain magazines and movies all highlight the successful development of sex into a major consumer industry.

In all this sex is presented as something to be consumed. But the sexual instinct differs from certain other instincts. Hunger can be satisfied by food. The 'food' of the sexual instinct is, however, another human being, capable of thinking, acting, suffering. The alienation of sexuality under the conditions of modern capitalism is very much part of the general alienating process, in which people are converted into objects (in this case objects of sexual consumption) and relationships are drained of human content. Undiscriminating, compulsive sexual activity is not sexual freedom — although it may sometimes be a preparation for it (which repressive morality can never be). The illusion that alienated sex is sexual freedom constitutes yet another obstacle on the road to total emancipation. Sexual freedom implies a realisation and understanding of the autonomy of others. Unfortunately, most people don't yet think in this way.

The recuperation by society of the sexual revolution is therefore partly successful. But it creates the basis for a deeper and more fundamental challenge. Modern society can tolerate alienated sexuality, just as it tolerates alienated consumption, wage increases which do not exceed increases in the productivity of labour, or colonial 'freedom' in which the 'facts of economic life' still perpetuate the division of the world into 'haves' and 'have not's. Modern capitalism not only tolerates these 'challenges' but converts them into essential cogs of its own expansion and perpetuation. It seeks to harness the sexual demands of youth by first distorting them and then by integrating them into the present system, in much the same way as working class demands are integrated into the economy of the consumer society. From a potential liberating force these demands tend thereby to be converted into a further mechanism of repression. What exploiting society will not long be able to tolerate, however, is the mass development of critical, demystified, self-reliant, sexually emancipated, autonomous, non-alienated persons, conscious of what they want and prepared to struggle for it.

The assertion of the right to manage one's own life, in the realm of sex as in the realm of work, is helping to disintegrate the dominant ideology. It is producing less compulsive and obsessional individuals, and in this respect preparing the ground for libertarian revolution. (In the long run even the traditional revolutionaries, that last repository of repressed puritanism, will be affected.)

The incessant questioning and challenge to authority on the traditional a revolutionaries, that last repository of repressed complement the questioning and challenge to authority in other areas (for instance on the subject of who is to dominate the work process — or of the purpose of work itself). Both challenges stress the autonomy of individuals and their domination over important aspects of their lives. Both expose the alienated concepts which pass for rationality and which govern so much of our thinking and behaviour. The task of the conscious revolutionary is to make both challenges explicit, to point out their deeply subversive content, and to explain their inter-relation. To understand revolutionary psychoanalysis is to add a new dimension to the marxist critique of ideologies and to the marxist understanding of false consciousness. Only then will we have the tools to master our own history, will socialism ('man's positive self-consciousness') be a real possibility, and will man be able to break once and for all with the 'irrational in politics' and with the irrational in life.

The Russian experience

In the years following the Revolution, 'official' thought and action concerning sexual matters were coloured by four main facts :

The novelty, depth and vast scale of the problems which the Bolsheviks had inherited. The new tasks had to be tackled at a time when innumerable other problems claimed urgent attention. In the struggle for sexual freedom classical marxist teaching provided no blueprint as to 'what was to be done'. Despite the vast social, intellectual and cultural turmoil, despite the widespread breaking up of families and despite the disintegration of many traditional values, there was no clear or coherent vision as to what ought eventually to follow.

This lack of conscious purpose was associated with a widespread, false, and rather naive belief that the abolition of economic exploitation and the promulgation of new, progressive legislation were sufficient to ensure the liberation of women. It was thought that this liberation (often conceived of in the restrictive sense of 'equal rights') would automatically follow the changes in the ownership of property and it was assumed that its growth would be guaranteed by the new laws and institutions of the 'workers' state'.

There was massive unawareness of the significance of sexual repression — and of the traditional morality based upon it — as a central factor in social conditioning. Only a small minority of revolutionaries saw a *conscious* sexual revolution as an essential component of total social change. Even fewer saw the sexual revolution as the indispensable means of deepening and completing the proposed social transformation, through changing the mental structure of the mass individual.

Among many of the Bolshevik leaders there was a gross lack of insight as to their own repressive conditioning in matters of sex and as to the impact this could be having on their thoughts and actions. Many had had a fairly typical authoritarian upbringing. Later, deportation, imprisonment and struggle under conditions of persecution and illegality had prevented most of the Old Guard from enjoying a normal sex life. After the Revolution a retrospective virtue was made out of what had been a historical necessity, and this 'dedication' was made an ideal not only for 'the vanguard' but for the masses themselves. Many leading Bolsheviks considered propaganda for sexual freedom as a 'division from the real struggle'. (So do many would-be Bolsheviks today!) Some of them were actively to oppose all attempts at such propaganda.

These various factors were to play their part in the series of internal defeats that followed the great events of 1917. They were to undermine important areas of human freedom, conquered in the first few months of the Revolution. The inhibition of the sexual revolution in Russia was to combine with other defeats (discussed at length elsewhere) [1] to reinforce the whole process of bureaucratic degeneration.

Classical Marxism contained little from which the Bolsheviks could have sought practical guidance. True, Engels had written passages with which no libertarian could quarrel.[2] But there were other passages, more doctrinaire in nature.[3] Moreover, Engels' historical analyses had constantly emphasised the social background against which the sexual revolution was to take place but had rarely dealt with the content of the process. As for Marx he had certainly stigmatised bourgeois marriage and the bourgeois family. He had mercilessly flayed the whole hypocrisy of bourgeois morality. But he had also denounced the 'movement counterposing universal private property to private property', a movement which 'finds expression in the bestial form of counterposing to marriage (certainly a form of exclusive private property) the community of women, in which a woman becomes a piece of communal and common property . . . ' If such a movement triumphed the woman would pass 'from marriage to general prostitution . . . from a relationship of exclusive marriage with the owner of private property to a state of universal prostitution with the community.[4] The terms are emotionally loaded and the antithesis suggested is a false one. (Marx still formulates the *alternative* to individual property in terms of property — and not in terms of the free self-determination of both men and women. It is in much the same vein that Engels still speaks of 'surrender').

(1.) See *'The Bolsheviks and Workers' Control 1917-1921'* by M. Brinton. Obtainable from Black Rose Books.

(2.) What we can conjecture at present about the regulation of sex relationships after the impending effacement of capitalist production is, in the main, of a negative character, limited mostly to what will vanish. But what will be added ? That will be settled after a new generation has grown up : a generation of men who never in all their lives have had occassion to purchase a woman's surrender either with money or with any other means of social power, and of women who have never been obliged to surrender to any man out of any consideration other than that of real love, or to refrain from giving themselves to their beloved for fear of the economic consequences. Once such people appear, they won't care a rap about what we today think they should do. They will establish their own practice and their own public opinion . . . and that's the end of it !' (F. Engels, *The Origin of the Family, Private Property and the State*. F.L.P.H., Moscow 1954, pp. 137-8.)

(3.) Describing for instance the effects of the industrial revolution which uprooted women from the home and drove them into factories, Engels says (in *The Condition of the Working Class in 1844*) that at times women even became the breadwinners while the husbands stayed at home as housekeepers. According to Engels this was 'an insane state of things' which 'unsexes the man and takes from the woman all womanliness'. The notion that woman's place is in the home has some strange advocates !

51

However ambiguous or indistinct the 'guide-lines' may have been in 1917 the problems requiring solution were real and practical enough. The cultural heritage of tsarism had to be uprooted. This was an enormous task. Tsarist laws had certainly 'protected' the family. They decreed that the husband 'had to love his wife like his own body'. The wife 'owed unlimited obedience to the husband'. Men could call on the police to compel women to return to the happy home. Parents could have their children of either sex confined to prison 'for wilfully disobeying parental power'. Young people contracting marriage without parental consent were also liable to imprisonment. Only religious marriages were deemed legal. Divorces, which only the Church could grant, were costly and only available to the rich.

All this reactionary legislation was swept aside by the new marriage decrees of December 19 and 20, 1917. These proclaimed the total equality of the contracting parties, an end to the legal incapacity of women, and the end of 'indissoluble' marriage through the ready availability of divorce. The husband was deprived of his prerogative of domination over the family. Women were given the right freely to determine their name, domicile and citizenship. Any man over the age of 18 (and any woman over the age of 16) could contract a marriage. As far as the offspring were concerned, no difference was recognised between 'natural parentage' and 'legal parentage'.

Divorce was made very easy. The only criterion was mutual agreement between the parties. When a partner wanted to relinquish a sexual companionship he did not have to 'give reasons'. Marriage and divorce became purely private matters. The registration of a relationship was not mandatory. Even when a relationship was registered, sexual relationships with others were not 'prosecuted'. (Not telling the partner about another relationship was, however, considered 'fraud'.) The obligation to pay alimony persisted for six months only after a separation, and only came into force if the partner was unemployed or otherwise incapable of earning a living. A law of 1919 legalised abortion during the first three months of pregnancy. All the old legislation directed against homosexuality amongst adults was repealed. Aspirations in this whole area of personal freedom are summarised by the jurist Hoichbarg, who wrote in the *Preface to the Bolshevik Marriage Code of 1919* that 'the institution of marriage carried within itself the seeds of its own destruction' and that 'the family still persisted only because we are dealing with socialism in a nascent state'.

(4.) K. Marx *Economic and Philosophical Manuscripts of 1844*. Published for F.L.P.H., Moscow, by Lawrence and Wishart, 1959, pp. 99-100.

The newly proclaimed laws were radical indeed. Writing in *Pravda* on September 15, 1919, Lenin could truthfully state that 'in the Soviet Republic not a stone remains of the laws which confined women to an inferior status'. Particularly degrading had been the laws 'which have deprived her of rights and which have often even humiliated her — that is to say the laws on divorce, the laws distinguishing natural from legitimate children, the laws demanding the determination of fatherhood before the upkeep of the child could be considered'. Lenin also seems to have been aware of the fact that 'laws were not enough' and that 'even when a full equality of rights has been achieved the oppression of women would continue'. But he saw this persisting oppression solely in terms of the domestic chores which for a while would still be her lot. 'In most cases such chores were the least productive, the most barbarous and the heaviest to fall on women's shoulders. For women to be totally free and the real equal of man household chores must be made a public responsibility and the women must participate in general production'.[5] Communal kitchens, creches and kindergartens — combined with access to all kinds of labour — were seen as the essential ingredients of woman's emancipation. 'The abolition of private property on the land and in the factories *alone* opens the road', wrote Lenin. 'to the total and real emancipation of woman'. Along this road there would be a 'transition from the small individual household to the big socialist household'.[6] This vision was undoubtedly shared by most of the leading Bolsheviks, who saw 'women's liberation' as the summated freedoms from economic slavery. The repressive mechanisms whereby female subjugation had become internalised in the minds of millions of women were not even suspected.

The new laws, it is true, provided a framework within which future attempts might be made, free from external constraints, at constructing human relationships of a new type. It is also true that the Bolsheviks wished to break patriarchal power. But they were only dimly aware of the role of the patriarchal family as the 'structure forming cell of class society[7] — as 'the structural and ideological place of reproduction of every social order based on authoritarian principles'.[8] Still less did they realise the role of sexual repression in perpetuating such important aspects of the dominant ideology as the compliance

---

(5.) In 1916 Lenin had denounced a capitalism which maintained woman as 'the slave of the household, imprisoned in the bedroom, the kitchen and the nursery'. (*Sochineniya*, XIX, pp. 232-233.)
(6.) *Pravda*, March 8, 1921.
(7.) W. Reich, *The Sexual Revolution*, p. 166.
(8.) Ibid., p. 157.

with authority and the fear of freedom. Had they been more conscious of these facts many practical problems would have been differently managed, many fruitless discussions by-passed, many retrogressive statements or acts avoided. The revolutionaries would have shown less tolerance with the spokesmen of the old ideology and morality, many of whom had been left in high positions, from where they were inflicting untold damage upon the developing cultural revolution. The Bolsheviks repeatedly stressed that the new laws were 'only a beginning'. But a beginning of what ? Wilhelm Reich points out that in the heated discussions of that period the conservatives seemed always to have the edge in all the arguments and the most ready access to all the 'proofs'. The revolutionaries 'were prepared neither theoretically nor practically for the difficulties which the cultural revolution brought with it'.[9] They knew little about the psychic structure of the generation they were seeking to win over from ideological allegiance to the Tsarist patriarchate. They were certainly trying to do something new. But they 'felt very clearly that they were not able to put this 'new' thing into words. They fought valiantly, but finally tired and failed on the discussion, partly because they themselves were caught in old concepts, from which they were unable to shake loose'.[10]

The Revolution encountered tremendous problems. The compulsive family had only been legally abolished. The attitudes on which it was based persisted. Economic difficulties persisted too. And 'as long as society could not guarantee security to all adults and adolescents this guarantee remained the function of the family.[11] The family therefore continued to exist. Its demands conflicted more and more with the new social obligations and aspirations of the group. The 'life-affirmative sexual relationships in the collectives' struggled against old family ties which 'pervaded every corner of everyday life and of the psychic structure'.[12] For instance 'parents, proletarians included, did not like to see their adolescent daughters go to meetings. They feared that the girl would 'go wrong' — that is start a sexual life. Though the children ought to go to the collective, the parents still made their old possessive demands on them. They were horrified when the children began to look at them with a critical eye'.[13] Even in the most radical circles girls could still be denounced as 'promiscuous', thererevealing the deep-seated residual moral condemnation of female

---

(9.) Ibid., p. 169-170.
(10.) Ibid., p. 168.
(11.) Ibid., p. 167.
(12.) Ibid., p. 160.
(13.) Ibid., p. 182.

sexuality underlying all the 'revolutionary' rhetoric.

The economic whip-hand of the patriarchal father over wife and children was certainly loosened. But the increased opportunities for sexual happiness did not as yet mean the psychic capacity to enjoy such happiness. The internalised constraints had barely been dented. Everything was still distorted by revealing the deep-seated residual moral condemnation of sexual habits persisted. Family members would drown out unconscious antagonism to one another with a forced affection and sticky dependence. 'One of the main difficulties was the inability of the women — genitally crippled and unprepared for economic independence as they were — to give up their slave-like protection of the family'[14] and the substitute gratification which they derived from their domination over the children. Those whose whole lives were sexually empty and economically dependent had made of the upbringing of children the be-all and end-all of their existence. It was difficult to combat these possessive tendencies and this misuse of power on the part of the mothers without real insight into their origin. The mothers fought bitterly against any restriction of these powers.

Everyday life proved much more conservative than economy mainly because it was a much less conscious process. The revolutionaries were not equipped — either ideologically or in terms of their own upbringing — to intervene effectively in the heated discussions that raged up and down the country of the 'sexual question'. There was no theory of the sexual revolution. Trotsky's pamphlet 'Problems of Life',[15] written in 1923, does not even mention the sexual question. Many Bolshevik leaders took refuge in the formula that 'sexuality was a private matter'. This was unfortunate and 'essentially an expression of the inability of the members of the Communist Party to manage the revolution in their own personal lives'. [16]

There was undoubtedly considerable malaise, at least to begin with. Many young people felt that these were important questions which should be honestly and openly talked about. Kollontai[17] gives some idea of what was being discussed. A functionary, Koltsov, points out that the key questions 'are never discussed. It is as if for some reason they were being avoided. I myself have never given them serious thought. They are new to me'. Another, Finkovsky, pin-points the reasons for this

(14.) Ibid., p. 160.
(15.) *Voprosy byta,* Moscow 1923. Translated by Z. Vengerova. English edition by Methuen, 1924.
(16.) W. Reich. *The Sexual Revolution,* p. 172.
(17.) A. Kollontai. *Novoya moral i rabochi klass* (The new morality and the working class), Moscow 1919, pp. 65, ff.

avoidance.'The subject is rarely talked about because it hits home too closely with everybody ... The Communists usually point to the golden future and thus avoid getting into acute problems ... the workers know that in Communist families things are even worse than in their own'. Yet another official, Tseitlin, stressed that these were 'exactly the questions which interest the workers, male and female alike'. When such questions were the topic of Party meetings people would hear about it and flock to attend them. 'They keep asking these questions and find no answers'. Reich points out that ordinary people, without sexological training or knowledge, were describing 'exactly what is contended by sex-economy', namely that 'the interest of the mass individual is not political but sexual'. [18]

Answers were in fact being provided. They were inadequate incomplete, and sometimes postively harmful. Sex 'education' was slipping into the hands of public hygienists, biologists, urologists and professors of philosophy, ethics and sociology. The repercussions soon began to be felt — the cultural revolution began to wither at the roots. The 'heated discussions' eventually died diwn. The impetus provided by the new legislation petered out — clearly revealing the obvious fact that a sexual revolution could not, like an economic revolution, be expressed through plans and laws. To be successful it had to manifest itself in all the details of everyday personal life. But here it encountered major obstacles. The revolution in the ideological superstructure had not yet taken place. The 'bearer of this revolution, the psychic structure of human beings',[19] was not yet changed.

Apart from the internalised inhibitions of the mass individual — a legacy from the past — change was also being inhibited from without (i.e. as result of the internalised inhibitions of those now in authority). Lenin denounced the youth movement as geing 'exaggeratedly concerned with sex'.[20] The youth had been 'attacked by the disease of modernity in its attitude towards sexual questions'. All this was 'particularly harmful, particularly dangerous'. The new 'flourishing sexual theories' arose out of the personal need of people 'to justify personal abnormality in sexual life before bourgeois morality'. They were being peddled by 'little yellow-beaked birds who had just broken from the egg of bourgeois ideas'. Psychoanalysis was to be mistrusted for it 'grew on the dirty soil of bourgeois society'. All that was relevant in this new concern with sexual matters 'the workers had already read in Bebel, long ago'. The new sexual life young

---

(18.) W. Reich. Op. cit., p. 174.
(19.) W. Reich. *The Sexual Revolution*, p. 159.

people were trying to create was 'an extension of bourgeois brothels'. Within a short while every timid official, every repressed reactionary was to be found echoing Lenin's famous phrase : 'Thirst must be satisfied — but will the normal man in normal circumstances lie down in the gutter and drink out of a puddle, or out of a glass with a rim greasy from many lips ? [21]

The more far-sighted among the revolutionaries sensed the backsliding. But their prescription was an intensification of the calls for industrialisation. The lack of the purely economic prerequisities for radical social change was stressed again and again. But as Reich points out the attitude 'first the economic questions, *then* those of everyday life' was wrong and only the expression of the unpreparedness for the seemingly chaotic forms of the cultural revolution ... True, a society which is exhausted by civil war, which is unable immediately to establish public kitchens, laundries and kindegartens must first of all think of the economic prerequisites ... But it was not just a matter of lifting the masses to the cultural level of the capitalist countries ... it was also necessary to be clear as to the nature of the new culture ... The cultural revolution posed infinitely more difficult problems than the political revolution. This is easy to understand. The political revolution requires essentially nothing but a strong trained leadership and the confidence of the masses in it. The cultural revolution, however, requires an alteration in the psychic structure of the mass individual. About this there was hardly any scientific, let alone practical, concept at that time'.[22] It might perhaps be added that the dissemination of what little knowledge there was, instead of being encouraged. was being actively opposed by most of the Russian leaders. Attempts at establishing various kinds of 'counter-milieu' — such as youth communes — were now also being actively discouraged by the authorities.

It was naive indeed to expect 'progressive' legislation plus was necessary and was precisely such a vision that was lacking.

---

(20) See Appendix to this book for source of various quotes from Lenin on the question of sex. The authenticity of Clara Zetkin's account has never been questioned. Her *'Reminiscences of Lenin'* have been produced many times by official Communist publishing houses, both in Russia and elsewhere.

(21) Lenin's metaphors concerning 'the gutter' and 'puddles' are revealing on two grounds. Implicit in them are a) the conception that sex is intrinsically dirty, and b) the conception that sex is a relationship with an object — water — rather than a relationship with another human being. The second point, it is true, is mitigated by Lenin's later statement that 'two lives are concerned ...' But the overall image was to be remembered long after the qualifying statement had been forgotten.

(22) W. Reich. *The Sexual Revolution,* p. 175-6.

The change in property relations may have prepared the ground for a new society but people alone were going to build it. For such a task a different kind of vision was necessary and it was precisely such a vision that was lacking.

Too many factors were combining to prevent the formal, legal changes that had been proclaimed from really influencing the course of events. As Reich was later to point out 'an ideology or programme can only become a revolutionary power of historical dimension if it achieves a deep reaching change in the emotions and instinctual life of the masses'. He clearly perceived that the famous 'subjective factor' in history was nothing 'but the psychic structure of the masses'. It influenced the development of society either 'by passively tolerating despotism and suppression' or 'by adjustement to the technical process of development instituted by the powers that be', or finally 'by actively taking part in social development, as for example in a revolution'. No concept of historical development could be called revolutionary 'if it considers the psychic structure of the masses as nothing but the result of economic processes and not *also* as their motive power'.[23] In the Russian Revolution the psychic structure of the masses never became — and was never allowed to become — a 'revolutionary power of historical dimensions'.

Between 1920 and about 1933 the situation gradually regressed to the point where the sexual ideology of the leading groups in the USSR could no longer be distinguished from that of the leading groups in any conservative country. Summing up the whole process Reich wrote that the leaders of the new Russian state could not be blamed for not knowing the solution to these problems, 'but they must be blamed for avoiding the difficulties, for taking the line of least resistance, for not asking themselves what it all meant, for talking about the revolution of life without looking for it in real life itself, for misinterpreting the existing chaos as a 'moral chaos' (using the terms in the same sense as the political reaction) instead of comprehending it as chaotic conditions which were inherent in the transition to new forms, and last but not least for repudiating the contributions to an understanding of the problem which the German sex-political movement hal to offer'.[24]

In March 1934 the law punishing homosexuality was reintroduced into the Soviet Union. In June 1935, an editorial in *Pravda* wrote that 'only a good family man could be a good Soviet citizen'. By early 1936 a Russian trade union paper (*Trud,*

---

(23) Ibid., p. 169.

April 27, 1936) could write 'abortion, which destroys life, is inadmissible in any country. Soviet woman has the same rights as Soviet man, but that does not absolve her from the great and honourable duty (sic !) imposed on her by nature : she is to be a mother. She is to bear life.[25] And this is certainly not a private matters, but a matter of great social significance.[26] A decree of June 27, 1936 was to prohibit abortion. A further decree of July 8, 1944 established that only a legally recognised marriage entailed rights and duties for both husband and wife'. In

---

(24) W. Reich. Ibid., p. 190.

(25) The myth that childbearing and rearing are the fulfilment of a woman's destiny is among the most pernicious and damaging myths that imprison her. It has harmful effects on the children themselves. The situation is well described in the following passage, taken from an article by Laurel Limpus, '*Liberation of Women, Sexual Repression and the Family*' obtainable from OUR GENERATION. 'Having children is no substitute for creating one's own life, for producing. And since so many women in this culture devote themselves to nothing else, they end up by becoming intolerable burdens upon their children because in fact these children *are* their whole lives. Juliet Mitchell ('*Women : the Longest Revolution*') has caught the situation exactly :

'At present, reproduction in our society is often a kind of sau mimicry of reproduction. Work in a capitalist society is an alienation of labour in the making of a social product which is confiscated by capital. But it can still sometime be a real act of creation, purposive and responsible, even in conditions of the worst exploitation. Maternity is often a caricature of this. The biological product —the child — is treated as if it were a solid product. Parenthood became a kind of substitute for work, an activity in which the child is seen as an object created by the mother, in the same way as a commodity is created by a worker. Naturally, the child does not literally escape, but the mother's alienation can be much worse than that of the worker whose product is appropriated by the boss. No human being can create another human being. A person's biological origin is an abstraction. The child as an autonomous person inevitably threatens the activity which claims to create it continually merely as a possession of the parent. Possessions are felt as extensions of the self. The child as a possession is supremely this. Anything the child does is therefore a threat to the mother herself who has renounced her autonomy through this misconception of her reproductive role. There are few more precarious ventures on which to base a life'.

'So we have the forty or fifty year old woman complaining to her grow child : 'But I gave you everything'. This is quite true : this is the tragedy. It is a gift the child hardly wanted, and indeed many children are daily mutilated by it. And it leaves women at the waning of their years with the feeling that they have been deceived, that their children are ungrateful, that no one appreaciates them because they have come to the realisation that they have *done* nothing'.

other words 'illegitimate' children — or the offspring of non-registered relationships — reverted to their earlier inferior status. Unmarried couples living together were urged to 'regularise their relationship. Divorce would only be allowed 'important cases' and after 'full' consideration of all the relevant facts by a special tribunal'. The cult of motherhood was given official blessing. An official stalinist publication [27] could boast that 'one June 1, 1949 in Soviet Russia, there were over 2 million mothers with families of 5 or 6 children who held the 'maternity medal'; 700,000 mothers of 7, 8, or 9 children holding the 'Glory to Motherhood' medal; and 30,000 mothers of 10 or more children entitled to the medal of 'Heroine Mother'. (Enough to warm the heart of the most reactionary of Popes!) The author proclaims that 'Soviet legislation on the question of the family has always been inspired by marxism-leninism, and that its evolution, over a 30-year period, had always had as its constant concern the wish to defend woman and to free her. This preoccupation had led the Soviet legislator from free divorce to regulated divorce and from legal abortion to the prohibition of abortion'!

From the middle thirties on, various critics of the bureaucracy had become increasingly vocal. Trotsky's book 'The Revolution Betrayed' first published in 1936, contains an interesting chapter on 'Family, Youth and Culture'. In it Trotsky stigmatised those who proclaimed that woman had to accept 'the joys of motherhood'. This was 'the philosophy of a priest endowed also with the powers of a gendarme'. Trotsky correctly points out that the 'problem of problems had not been solved : the forty million Soviet families remained in their overwhelming majority nests of medievalism, female slavery and hysteria, daily humiliation of children, feminine and childish superstition'. 'The most compelling motive of the present cult of the family (was) undoubtedly the need of the bureaucracy for a stable hierarchy of relations and for the disciplining of youth by means of forty million points of support for authority and power'. The description is excellent. What is lacking is any real understanding of how it all came about. Economic and cultural backwardness are still seen as the sole ingredients of the failure. A whole dimension is missing. The role of Bolshevik obscurantism in relation to sex is not even suspected. One would search in vain among

---

(26) In his *Principles of Communism* Engels had written that the socialist revolution 'would transform the relations between the sexes into purely private relations, only concerning the people participating in them and in which society had not to intervene'.

(27) *La femme et la communiste,* Editions Sociales, Paris 1951.

Trotsky's voluminous writings for any criticism, however muted, of what Lenin had said on the subject.

In the last twenty years — despite a steady 'development of the productive forces' — the sexual counter-revolution has gained even further momentum. The distance travelled is perhaps best epitomised in a book by T.S. Atarov, 'Physician Emeritus of the Russian Soviet Socialist Republic'. The book, published in Moscow in 1959, is called *'Problems of Sexual Education'*, [28] and reveals the full extent of the sexual Thermidor. The author proclaims that 'Soviet marriage is not only not a private matter. It is a question involving society and the State'. Young people are denounced who have pre-martial intercourse 'without even experiencing guilt'. 'Unadapted elements' in Russian society are denounced, who had even sought to give 'philosophical expression' to their attitude — in other words who had sought to argue a coherent case against the sexually repressive ideology of the Party leaders. Atarov bemoans the fact that young people 'don't seem to realise the difference between puberty and sexual maturity' and that they seem to believe 'that the mere existence of sexual desire is a justification for its satisfaction'. But there were also encouraging signs. 'Under Soviet conditions masturbation is no longer the mass phenomenon it was in the past'. But 'unfortunately it still persisted. According to Atarov, various factors tended to perpetuate this alarming state of affairs, factors such as 'tight fitting clothing in the nether parts, the bad habits of boys who keep their hands in their pockets [29] or under their blankets or who lie on their stomachs, constipation and full bladders, the reading of erotic books and the contemplation of the sexual activity of animals'.

How was one to fight this menace to the stability of Russian society ? Yes ! How did you guess ? 'Regular meals, hard beds, exercise, walking, sport and gymnastics, in fact anything that will deflect the child's attention from sexual preoccupations'.

---

(28) For detailed review, see article on 'Sexual Thermidor' in *SOLIDARITY* (North London), vol. 4, no. 8. A few copies are still available.
(29) Lenin had also spoken (see Appendix I) of 'healthy sport, swimming, racing, walking, bodily exercises of every kind' as giving young people more than 'eternal theories and discussions about sexual problems'. 'Healthy bodies, healthy minds', he said, echoing the words of Juvenal ('mens sana in corpore sano', *Satires*, 10, 356), the Stoic moralist and misogynist who had 'exposed the vices' of ancient Rome.

Discussing menstruation Atarav is even more with it ! 'Under no circumstances should any cotton or gauze appliance be inserted into the vagina as so many women do'. The 'outer parts' should be washed twice a day with warm boiled water. Our political spinter advises that 'young people should be forbidden from serving in cafes, restaurants or bars for the atmosphere in these places encourages them to indulge in pre-marital relation'. 'No illness'. he stresses, 'was ever caused through abstinence, which is quite harmless for young and less young alike'. In a frightening phrase Atarov sums up the spirit of his book. 'The law cannot concern itself with every case of immoral conduct. The pressure of public opinion must continue to play the leading role against all forms of immorality'. The vice squad and public opinion were again to be the pillars of the sexual Establishment.

Readers will grasp the deeply reactionary significance of Atarov's pronouncements, particularly when endorsed by the whole might of the Russian Educational Establishment (over 100,000 copies of Atarov's book were sold within a few days of the publication of the first edition). The 'public opinion' which Atarov refers to is the one which had sought emancipation for a short while after 1917, but had soon been dragged back into the old rut of bigotry and repression. It could now be used again for censorious ends — as it had been for generations in the past.

Official Russian sexual morality — as seen through other official works — today resembles the kind of 'advice to parents' dished out about 1890 by the bourgeois do-gooders of that time.[30] One finds in it all the fetishes of bourgeois sexual morality — or more generally of all systems of morality characterising class societies of patriarchal type. Everything is there : all the reactionary, anti-life ideas pompously disguised as 'science' every backward prejudice, all the hypocritical bad faith of screwed-up and repressed puritans. But these 'irrational' ideas not only have definite social roots (which we have sought to expose). They also have a precise significance and a specific function. In this they closely resemble the repressive morality with those who symbolise authority, with those who incarnate — Church-dominated Western countries.

---

(30) Much contemporary sexological Russian literature reads like the works of Baden Powell, founder of the Boy Scouts, but with the word 'socialism' occasionally scattered among the references to 'duty', 'loyalty', 'discipline', 'service' and 'patriotism'.

Both East and West these ideologies aim at denying to individuals the autonomous (i.e. the conscious and self-managing) exercise of their own activities. They aim at depriving people of freedom and responsibility in a fundamental realm and at obliging them to conform to externally imposed norms and to the pressures of 'public opinion' rather than to criteria determined by each person according to his own needs and experience. The objective of these repressive and alienating moralities is the mass creation of individuals whose character structure complements and reinforces the hierarchical structure of society. Such individuals will accept 'irrational' norms, because they have internalised the dictates of an 'irrational' society, dictates which are essential to the perpetuation of that society. Such individuals will revert to infantile attitudes when confronted with those who symbolise authority, with those incarnate — at the scale of society — the image of their parent (i.e. rulers of the state, managers of industry, priests, political pundits, etc.). In the Russian context they will comply with the edicts of the Central Committee, obediently follow the zig-zags of the Party line, develop religious attitudes to the Holy Writings, etc. Such individuals will also react in an anxiety-laden manner when confronted with deviants of all kinds (perceptive writers, poets, cosmopolitans, the apostles of 'modernity', those with long hair and those with long ideas). It is really surprising that the most sexually repressed segment of the Russian population (obese, middle-aged women) still seem to be the main vehicle for the dissemination of 'public opinion' and the prevailing 'kulturnost'[31] — despite the nationalisation, nearly two generations ago, of the vast majority of the means of production?

---

(31) See *SOLITARITY* (North London), vol. 6, no 3, for a description of these attempts to enforce this 'behaviour expected of cultured people'.

APPENDIX 1

REMINISCENCES of LENIN by Clara Zetkin

Lenin seldom talked about sex. Stripped of their 'revolutionary' rhetoric his occasional pronouncements on the subject were those of a puritan bigot.

Because of Lenin's eminence and authority in other fields his views on sex exerted considerable influence. They were seized upon and repeated ad nauseam by all those opposed to any radical change in the field of sex relations. In this sense they played a significant role in the sexual counter-revolution which we have sought to outline in this book.

We here publish an excerpt from the chapter 'Women, Marriage and Sex' of Clara Zetkin's book 'Reminiscences of Lenin'. [1] The book was written in 1924, shortly after Lenin's death. Zetkin, a founding member of the German Communist Party, is speaking to Lenin in the Kremlin, in the autumn of 1920.

Lenin continued : 'Your list of sins, Clara, is still longer. I was told that questions of sex and marriage are the main subjects dealt with in the reading and discussion evenings of women comrades. They are the chief subject of interest, of political instruction and education. I could scarcely believe my ears when I heard it. The first country of proletarian dictatorships surrounded by the counter-revolutionaries of the whole world, the situation in Germany itself requires the greatest possible concentration of all proletarian, revolutionary forces to defeat the ever-growing and ever-increasing counter-revolution. But working women comrades discuss sexual problems and the question of forms of marriage in the past, present and future. They think it their most important duty to enlighten proletarian women on these subjects. The most widely read brochure is, I believe, the pamphlet of a young Viennese woman comrade on the sexual proplem. What a waste ! What truth there is in it the workers have already read in Bebel, long ago. Only not so boringly, not so heavily written as in the pamphlet, but written strongly, bitterly, aggressively, against bourgeois society.

'The extension on Freudian hypotheses seems 'educated', even scientific, but it is ignorant, bungling. Freudian theory is the modern fashion. I mistrust the sexual theories of the articles, dissertations, pamphlets, etc., in short, of that particular kind of literature which flourishes luxuriantly in the dirty soil of bourgeois society. I mistrust those who are always contemplating the several questions, like the Indian saint his navel. It seems to me these flourishing sexual theories which are mainly hypothetical, and often quite arbitrary hypotheses, arise from the personal need to justify personal abnormality or hypertrophy in sexual life before bourgeois morality, and to entreat its patience. This masked respect for bourgeois morality seems to me just as repulsive as poking about in sexual matters. However wild and revolutionary the behavior may be, it is still really quite bourgeois. It is, mainly, a hobby of the intellectuals and of the sections nearest them. There is no place for it in the Party, in the class conscious, fighting proletariat'.

I interrupted here, saying that the questions of sex and marriage, in a bourgeois society of private property, involve many problems, conflicts and much suffering for women of all social classes and ranks. The war and its consequences had greatly accentuated the conflicts and sufferings of women in sexual matters, had brought to light problems which were formerly hidden from them. To that were added the effects of

---

1. International Publishers, New York 1934, pp. 44-51.

the revolution. The old world of feeling and thought had begun to totter. Old social ties are entangling and breaking, there are the tendencies towards new ideological relationships between man and woman. The interest shown in these questions is an expression of the need for enlightenment and reorientation. It also indicates a reaction against the falseness and hypocrisy of bourgeois society. Forms of marriage and the family, in their historical development and dependence upon economic life, are calculated to destroy the superstition existing in the minds of working women concerning the eternal character of bourgeois society. A critical, historical attitude to those problems must lead to a ruthless examination of bourgeois society, to a disclosure of its real nature and effects, including condemnation of its sexual morality and falseness. All roads lead to Rome. And every real Marxist analysis of any important section of the ideological superstructure of society, of a predominating social phenomenon, must lead to an analysis of bourgeois society and of its property basis, must end in the realisation, 'this must be destroyed'.

Lenin nodded laughingly. 'There we have it! You are defending counsel for your women comrades and your Party. Of course what you say is right. But it only excuses the mistakes made in Germany; it does not justify them. They are, and remain, mistakes. Can you really seriously assure me that the questions of sex and marriage were discussed from the standpoint of a mature, living, historical materialism? Deep and many-sided knowledge is necessary for that, the clearest Marxist mastery of a great amount of material. Where can you get the forces for that now? If they existed, then pamphlets like the one I mentioned would not be used as material for study in the reading and discussion circles. They are distributed and recommended, instead of being criticised. And what is the result of this futile, un-Marxist dealing with the question? That questions of sex and marriage are understood not as part of the large social question? No, worse! The great social question appears as an adjunct, a part, of sexual problems. The main thing becomes a subsidiary matter. That does not only endanger clarity on that question itself, it muddles the thoughts, the class consciousness of proletarian women generally.

'Last and not least. Even the wise Solomon said that everything has its time. I ask you: Is now the time to amuse proletarian women with discussions on how one loves and is loved, how one marries and is married? Of course, in the past, present and future, and among different nations — what is proudly called historical materialism! Now all thoughts of women comrade, of the women of the working people, must be directed towards the proletarian revolution. It creates the basis for a real renovation in marriage and sexual relations. At the moment other problems are more urgent than the marriage forms of Maoris or incest in olden times. The question of Soviets is still on the agenda for the German proletariat. The Versailles Treaty and its effect on the life of the working woman — unemployment, falling wages, taxes, and a great deal more. In short, I maintain that this kind of political, social education for proletarian women is false, quite, quite false. How could you be silent about it ? You must use your authority against it'.

I have not failed to criticise and remonstrate with leading women comrades in the separate districts, I told my angry friend. He himself knew that a phophet is never recognised in his own country or family. By my criticism I had laid myself open to the charge of 'strong survivals of social democratic ideology and old-fashioned Philistinism'. But at last the criticism had begun to take effect. Questions of sex and marriage were no longer the central feature of discussion. But Lenin continued the thread of thought further.

'I know, I know', he said. 'I have also been accused by many people of Philistinism in this matter, although that is repulsive to me. There is so much hypocrisy and narrow-mindedness in it. Well, I'm bearing it calmly ! The little yellow-beaked birds who have just broken from the egg of bourgeois ideas are always frightfully clever. We shall have to let that go. The youth movement too is attacked with the disease of modernity in its attitude towards sexual questions and in being exaggeratedly concerned with them'. Lenin gave an ironic emphasis to the word modernity and grimaced as he did so. 'I have been told that sexual questions are the favorite study of your youth organisations, too. There is supposed to be a lack of sufficient orators on the subject. Such misconceptions are particularly harmful, particularly dangerous in the youth movement. They can very easily contribute towards over-excitement and exaggeration in the sexual life of some of them, to a waste of youthful health and strength. You must fight against that, too. There are not a few points of contact between the women's and youth movements. Our women comrades must work together systematically with the youth. That is a continuation, an extension and exaltation of motherliness from the individual to the social sphere. And all the awakening social life and activity of women must be encouraged, so that they can discard the limitations of their Philistine individualist home and family psychology. But we'll come to that later.

'With us, too, a large part of the youth is keen on 'revising bourgeois conceptions and morality' concerning sexual questions. And, I must add, a large part of our best, our most promising young people. What you said before is true. In the conditions created by the war and the revolution the old ideological values disappeared or lost their binding force. The new values are crystalising slowly, in struggle. In the relations between man and man, between man and woman, feelings and thoughts are becoming revolutionised. New boundaries are being set up between the rights of the individual and the rights of the whole, in the duties of individuals. The matter is still in a completely chaotic ferment. The direction, the forces of development in the various contradictory tendencies are not yet clearly defined. It is a slow and often a very painful process of decay and growth. And particularly in the sphere of sexual relationships, of marriage and the family. The decay, the corruption, the filth of bourgeois marriage, with its difficult divorce, its freedom for the man, its enslavement for the woman, the repulsive hypocrisy of sexual morality and relations fill the most active minded and best people with deep disgust. ...

'The changed attitude of the young people to questions of sexual life is of course based on a 'principle' and a theory. Many of them call their attitude 'revolutionary' and 'Communistic'. And they honestly believe that it is so. That does not impress us old people. Although I am nothing but a gloomy ascetic, the so-called 'new sexual life' of the youth — and sometimes of the old — often seems to me to be purely bourgeois, an extension of bourgeois brothels. That has nothing whatever in common with freedom of love as we Communists understand it. You must be aware of the famous theory that in Communist society the satisfaction of sexual desires, of love, will be as simple and unimportant as drinking a glass of water. This glass of water theory has made our young people mad, quite mad. It has proved fatal to many young boys and girls. Its adherents maintain that it is Marxist. But thanks for such Marxism which directly and immediately attributes all phenomena and changes in the ideological superstructure of society to its economic basis ! Matters aren't quite as simple as that. A certain Frederick Engels pointed that out a long time ago with regard to historical materialism.

'I think this glass of water theory is completely un-Marxist, and moreover, anti-social. ... Of course, thirst must be satisfied. But will the normal man in normal circumstances lie down in the gutter and drink out of a puddle, or out of a glass with a rim greasy from many lips ? But the social aspect is most important of all. Drinking water is of course an individual affair. But in love two lives are concerned, and a third, a new life, arises. It is that which gives it its social interest, which gives rise to a duty towards the community.

'As a communist I have not the least sympathy for the glass of water theory, altought it bears the fine title 'satisfaction of love'. In any case, this liberation of love is neither new. nor Communist. You will remember that about the middle of the last century it was preached as the 'emancipation of the heart' in romantic literature. In bourgeois practice it became the emancipation of the flesh. At that time the preaching was more talented than it is today, and as for the practice, I cannot judge. I don't mean to preach asceticism by my criticism. Not in the least. Communism will not bring asceticism, but joy of life, power of life, and a satisfied love life will help to do that. But in my opinion the present widespread hypertrophy in sexual matters does not give joy and force to life, but takes it away. In the age of revolution that is bad, very bad.

'Young people, particularly, need the joy and force of life. Healthy sport, swimming, racing, walking, bodily exercises of every kind, and many-sided intellectual interests. Learning, studying, inquiry, as far as possible in common. That will give young people more than eternal theories and discussions about sexual problems and the so-called 'living to the full'. Healthy bodies, healthy minds ! Neither monk nor Don Juan, nor the intermediate attitude of the German Philistines. You know young comrade --- ? A splendid boy, and highly talented. And yet I fear that nothing good will come out of him. He reels and staggers from one love affair to the next. That won't do for the political struggle, for the revolution. And I wouldn't bet on the reliability, the endurance in struggle of those women who confuse their personal romances with politics. Nor on the men who run after every petticoat and get entrapped by every young woman. No, no ! that does not square with the revolution'.

Lenin sprang up, banged his hand on the table, and paced the room for a while.

'The revolution demands concentration, increase of forces. From the masses, from individuals. It cannot tolerate orgiastic conditions, such as are normal for the decadent heroes and heroines of D'Annunzio. Dissoluteness in sexual life is bourgeois, is a phenomenon of decay. The proletariat is a rising class. It doesn't need intoxication as a narcotic or a stimulus. Intoxication as little by sexual exaggeration as by alcohol. It must not and shall not forget, forget the shame, the filth, the savagery of capitalism. It receives the strongest urge to fight from a class situation, from the Communist ideal. It needs clarity, clarity and again clarity. And so I repeat, no weakening, no waste, no destruction of forces. Self-control, self-discipline is not slavery,

69

not even in love. But forgive me, Clara, I have wandered far from the starting point of our conversation. Why didn't you call me to order ? My tongue has run away with me. I am deeply concerned about the future of our youth. It is a part of the revolution. And if harmful tendencies are appearing, creeping over from bourgeois society into the world of revolution — as the roots of many weeds spread — it is better to combat them early. Such questions are part of the women question'.

APPENDIX 2

MEMOIRS OF A REVOLUTIONARY
by Victor Serge

Victor Serge's writings contain many vivid passages describing what it was like to live in Russia immediately after the Revolution. The following excerpt, describing events in Leningrad in 1926, is taken from Serge's major work *'Memoirs of a Revolutionary 1901-1941'* (Oxford Paperback 1967, pp. 205-207).

'**The** calm of the workers' city of Leningrad was suddenly broken by the dramatic incident of Chubarov Alley, which shed a sinister light on the conditions under which our youth lived. About fifteen young workers from the San-Galli works had raped an unfortunate girl, the same age as they, on a piece of waste ground near the October railway station. This took place in the Ligovka quarter, a district where the underworld and the working class met, full of scabby tenements. The Party's Control Commission, now overloaded with nasty little morals-cases, had a sort of epidemic of collective rapes to investigate. Doubtless sexuality, so long repressed, first by revolutionary asceticism and then poverty and famine, was beginning to recover its drive in a society that had been abruptly cut off from any spiritual nourishment. Promiscuity fed upon misery of the environment.

'The fifteen defendants from Chubarov Alley were given a showtrial in a workers' club-room, with the portrait of Lenin overlooking all. Rafail, the editor of the Leningrad *Pravda*, presided ; he was a tame, crafty-looking, bald official. At no moment did he give the slightest indication of understanding the tangled complexity of human baseness and poverty-induced corruption that it was his task to unravel in the name of working class justice. A hall full of men and women workers followed the cross-examination in an atmosphere of suspenseful boredom. The accused fifteen had the typical faces of Ligovka gutter-kids, fusing the peasant and proletarian types with primitive brutality as their salient feature. They offered confessions and denounced one another with no inhibitions about giving details. If ever the case diverged from the strictly factual they could not follow it, and found it all a great fuss to be made over things that often just pass by without any bother. What was more natural than sex on waste sites ? And what if she didn't mind mating with four, five or six? She would have got just as pregnant or diseased if it had only been one. And if she did mind, perhaps it's because she had 'prejudices'.

'Certain parts of the cross-examination are still clear in my memory. The lack of any insight on the part of the accused was so primitive in its quality that the magistrate Rafail, good committeeman that he was, was continually put out by it. He had just been so foolish as to talk of 'new culture' and 'our wonderful Soviet morals'. A short, fair-haired lad with a flat nose answered him :

'Never heard of 'em.'

Rafail went on, 'Of course, you'd prefer foreign bourgeois morals, wouldn't you ?'

It was ridiculous, it was horrible. The boy replied, 'I don't know nothing about them. Me, 'I've never been abroad.'

'You could have got to know about them through reading foreign newspapers.'

'I never even see Soviet newspapers. The Ligovka streets, that's the only culture I know.'

Five of the accused were condemned to death. In order to be able to carry out the sentence, the authorities had to twist the law and accuse them of 'banditry'. On the evening of the verdict, the sky above the city glowed purple. I walked towards the glow : the whole of the San-Galli works was in flames. The five condemned youths were executed on the following day. There was a rumour that the workers who had started the fire had been executed secretly, but this was impossible to confirm'.

THE KRONSTADT UPRISING

*by Ida Mett
with a preface by
Murray Bookchin*

The full story at last of the monumental 1921 events: the first workers' uprising against the Soviet bureaucracy. This book contains hitherto unavailable documents and a bibliography.

The book is in effect a different kind of history. It is written from a perspective that is concerned with the *people* as the primary social force in changing society and not leaders, conventions, manifestos and the like.

Murray Bookchin puts this recently translated book from the French into its contemporary setting.

100 pages / Paperback $1.45
ISBN : 0-919618-13-8

BLACK ROSE BOOKS No. B3

THE STATE : Its Historic Role
BY PETER KROPOTKIN

This anarchist classic, long out of print and still in great demand was first to be delivered as a lecture in Paris in March 1896. Kropotkin however, when he landed in France on his way from London was refused entry. The book develops the thesis of how the State grew over decades into its modern form. It deals in particular with the conflict between the free cities in the Middle Ages and the growing power of central states.
021/56 pages   **Paperback $1.75**

ABC OF ANARCHISM
BY ALEXANDER BERKMAN

This classic has also been out of print for some time. First published in 1929, and again in 1936, 1942, 1945, 1964, 1968 it has a very wide appeal. This edition has a new introduction by Peter Newell. The book deals with such questions as — Is Anarchism Violence ? What is Anarchism? Is Anarchy Possible ? Will Communist Anarchism Work ? Why Revolution ? The Idea is the Thing, Preparation, Organisation of Labour, Principles and Practice, Consumption and Exchange, Production, and Defence.
022/86 pages   **Paperback $1.75**

THE BOLSHEVIKS AND WORKERS' CONTROL 1917-21
BY MAURICE BRINTON

Workers' control is again widely discussed and widely researched. This book has two aims. It seeks to contribute new factual material to the current discussion on workers' control. And it attempts a new kind of analysis of the fate of the Russian Revolution. The two objectives, as will be shown, are inter-related.

An impressive array of documentation is brought to bear on how the Bolshevik State related to the whole question of self-management in revolutionary Russia. Sources are used which have never before been so inter-related and interpreted within such a profound analysis. This book has great significance today especially for those who are interested in a historical understanding of the question of a democracy of participation and popular control.
02/100 pages   **Paperback $1.75**

ESSAYS ON MARX'S THEORY OF VALUE

by Issaak Illich Rubin

According to the prevailing theories of economists, economics has replaced political economy, and economics deals with scarcity, prices, and resource allocation. In the definition of Paul Samuelson, "economics — or political economy, as it used to be called ... is the study of how men and society *choose,* with or without the use of money, to employ *scarce* productive resources, which could have alternative uses, to produce various commodities over time and distribute them for consumption, now and in the future, among various people and groups in society."

If economics is indeed merely a new name for political economy, and if the subject matter which was once covered under the heading of political economy is now covered by economics, then economics has replaced political economy. However, if the subject matter of political economy is not the same as that of economics, then the "replacement" of political economy is actually an omission of a field of knowledge. If economics answers different questions from those raised by political economy, and if the omitted questions refer to the form and the quality of human life within the dominant social-economic system, then this omission can be called a "great evasion".

Economic theorist and historian I. I. Rubin suggested a definition of political economy which has nothing in common with the definition of economics quoted above. According to Rubin, "Political economy deals with human working activity, not from the standpoint of its technical methods and instruments of labor, but from the standpoint of its social form. It deals with *production relations* which are established among people in the process of production." In terms of this definition, political economy is not the study of prices or of scarce resources; it is a study of social relations, a study of culture.

Rubin's book was first published in the Soviet Union, and was never re-issued after 1928. This is the first and only English edition. The translators are Milos Samardzija and Fredy Perlman.

275 pages/Hardcover : $7.50   ISBN : 0-919618-11-1

THE POLITICAL ECONOMY OF THE STATE

Canada/Québec/USA

edited by
Dimitrios Roussopoulos

This new book subjects the State in our society to a rigourous examination. Both the enormous growth of the State bureaucracy and the myth of its neutrality in social and economic affairs is carefully studied. Rick Deaton in *"The Fiscal Crisis of the State in Canada"*, deals with the whole range of activities in the public sector as well as the enormous growth of the Federal State, while B. Roy Lemoine in *"The Growth of the State in Québec"* examines the new role and function of the State since the "quiet revolution". Graeme Nicholson in *"Authority and the State"* studies the relationship of authoritarian patterns of behaviour and hierachical institutions which are inter-laced with the State at their highest expression, while John and Margaret Rowntree in *"Revolution in the Metropolis"* submit a major essay that pulls many of the themes of the book together. Finally Lorne Huston comments on the effect of *Local Initiative Projects* and *Opportunities for Youth* grants on citizens groups.

The Political Economy of the State begins an important new approach to the study of government and society which political science has ignored for a very long time.

200 pages / Hardcover $9.95 / Paperback $2.95
ISBN : 0-919618-02 / ISBN : 0-919618-01-4